DARTMOOR CENTURY II

DARTMOOR CENTURY II

Photographs from the Taylor Collection 1890-1970

Simon Butler

Contemporary photographs 2000–2001
by John Earle and Bryan Harper

HALSGROVE • DEVON BOOKS
PUBLISHED IN ASSOCIATION
WITH THE DARTMOOR TRUST

First published in Great Britain in 2001

British Library Cataloguing-in-Publication Data
A CIP record for this title is available from the British Library

1 85522 783 5

DEVON BOOKS
OFFICIAL PUBLISHER TO DEVON COUNTY COUNCIL

in association with

HALSGROVE
PUBLISHING, MEDIA AND DISTRIBUTION

Halsgrove House
Lower Moor Way
Tiverton, Devon EX16 6SS
Tel: 01884 243242
Fax: 01884 243325
email sales@halsgrove.com
website www.halsgrove.com

Printed and bound in Great Britain by Bookcraft Ltd, Midsomer Norton

Contents

Four Victorians sit amid the new-mown hay on a superb summer's day outside their home. This is one of the few, as yet, unidentified photographs from the Taylor Collection. As this and other images in the collection become more widely accessible so further information concerning them will inevitably emerge.

(TayBB55)

For there's them that Do
And them that Whine
And I know which I'd rather be.
For Greeveance is a fool's past-time
When making Historie.

Col. James Butler. *Letters*, 1646

Foreword

The preservation of Dartmoor is of importance to many people, and particularly to those who have known it from childhood. To ensure the future of Dartmoor it is necessary to understand its past. The archive which is being set up by the Dartmoor Trust plays an important part in fostering this understanding.

The photographs in this book, the accompanying exhibition, and the digitisation of the Taylor Collection, result directly from the work of the Dartmoor Trust and its members, whose efforts are to be applauded.

Quite apart from these long term aims there is a more immediate reason for being pleased that these photographs are now more widely on view. Quietly watching those who attended the original Dartmoor Century exhibition one was struck by the personal memories and recollections inspired by each photograph. In front of every picture groups of people stopped to share their experiences and memories. Others enjoyed a moment or two of quiet reflection.

On many occasions during my childhood I recall watching the steam engines come and go at Yelverton station. As the photographs of that railway line included in this book reveal, what seemed so permanent a part of our lives then has now faded almost completely.

Such memories are important to us all, not only personally, but to ensure that we pass on to future generations the lessons and experiences of the past.

Lady Kitson
February 2001

ACKNOWLEDGEMENTS

First thanks are to the Taylor family whose members diligently captured images of Dartmoor that form the collection on which this book is based. To Robin Fenner particular thanks are due, for without him the collection may never have found its way into public hands. For their agreement to the digitisation of the collection, and the use of the images in this book and exhibition, thanks go to the Devon Library Service, particularly Ian Maxted, and to Tess Walker of the Dartmoor National Park Authority, for it was she who devoted her time to the care and indexing of the original negatives. Peter Hamilton-Leggett has, as ever, helped with a will whenever asked.

No one has worked harder (or in worse weather), than John Earle and Bryan Harper who gave their time freely to photograph the present-day scenes complementing the Taylor pictures. Bryan has also worked tirelessly to produce the framed images for the exhibition. Their work and that of all other members of the Trust in supporting this book is much appreciated.

The Dartmoor National Park Authority has supported this project through-out, not least in providing exhibition space at the High Moorland Visitor Centre in Princetown. Head of Communications, John Weir, his colleagues Kerenza Townsend and Mike Nendick, have all been most helpful, as have the DNP Information staff at Princetown: Barbara, Sarah, Bob, Jim, Roger, Wendy, Margaret and Jean, whose help in identifying places in the photographs has been invaluable.

The works of many contemporary authors have been consulted and quoted. Thanks are due to them and to their publishers. They include Jeremy Butler, Stephen Woods, Eric Hemery, Reg Bellamy, Pauline Hemery, Roy and Ursula Radford, and Dick Wills, along with many others.

A number of people whose properties appear in the photographs have offered useful information and, without exception, have welcomed our approach. They include Mr Collins and family at Higher Mill, Peter Tavy, Brian Salt of Buckland Monachorum, Mr M.J. Cunliffe at Okehampton, Margaret Duffy of Dousland, Norman Scott of Shilston Farm, and those unnamed who kindly posed for the photographs without complaint!

Finally thanks to all those who supported the original exhibition and book. Their many kind comments and support for the Dartmoor Trust and its work is greatly appreciated.

Preface

BY THE CHAIRMAN OF THE DARTMOOR TRUST

In my introduction to the first book *Dartmoor Century* I wrote that those involved in the establishment of the Dartmoor Trust 'believed that it was important to proceed with caution; the objective being to lay down some firm foundations. Our shared vision has always been the creation of an organisation that will grow over a period of years to become a body bringing real benefits to Dartmoor.' This vision remains strong today.

A cautious approach, however, does not mean that the Trust has not moved forward and, indeed, a great deal of further work has been done towards the creation of an archive for Dartmoor. A feasibility study has been completed, consultation with a large number of professional and public organisations undertaken, and a bid prepared seeking funding in order to establish a three-year programme of work that will see the first stages of a photographic archive firmly in place.

The opening of the Dartmoor Century II exhibition and the publication of this book, along with the completed digitisation of the Taylor Collection, provide an opportunity to celebrate our work so far, and to look forward to taking our first steps in setting up the Dartmoor Archive.

It gives me an enormous amount of pleasure to see the aims of the Dartmoor Trust coming to fruition, and I congratulate all those who have worked so very hard to achieve it.

Philip R Sanders
Chairman of The Dartmoor Trust

"Photography's most basic reality is that it shows us the past. Whether we view a freshly made instant picture taken at a family picnic, or a very old one... they all inevitably look backwards through time. One result of this photographic fact is that we can see a record of how things have changed, and so the picture takes on some of the role of the fossil paleontologist; it can provide evidence of intermediate forms that existed during an evolutionary process..."

A Maritime Album
Szarkowski and Benson
Yale University Press, 1997

Members of the Taylor family under the bough of a wayside oak tree in Coppicetown Lane, Yelverton, Whitsun 1914.

(TayG141)

Introduction

This work has been published as a direct result of the success of the book and exhibition of photographs produced in April 2000 under the title *Dartmoor Century*. The exhibition, opened at the High Moorland Visitor Centre in Princetown in April 2000, drew in thousands of people and received almost universal plaudits both for the intrinsic quality of the photographs on show, and for the overall aims of the Dartmoor Trust in establishing an archive for Dartmoor. Of course it should not be overlooked that Robert Burnard's photographs of which the exhibition was comprised are so delightful that it would be hard to fail to please, but there was clearly more to the exhibition's success than that. In fact what people appeared most to enjoy was the juxtaposition of Burnard's photographs taken a hundred years ago with those showing the scene taken a century later.

Of course, while part of intent of the exhibition was to spark a debate over the changes (or lack of them) between the scenes in each of the pair of images, a further and unexpected result was viewers' enthusiastic personal responses to the pictures on show: for instance a photograph of Burnard's family at Postbridge brought back to many viewers memories of *their* family picnics beside the Dart in summers long past. Thus each photograph threw open a welcome window on our individual past lives.

It is this response as much as any other which has stimulated this further publication and a second exhibition. Indeed the public's enthusiasm for that first exhibition and book has led directly to its successor, for the royalties generated from sales have paid for the digital archiving of the Taylor Collection from which this new selection of photographs is drawn (about which more follows in a later chapter). Thus, apart from the principal aim of the Trust in establishing an archive for Dartmoor, a hidden and hitherto unguessed at benefit has arisen – that of making the superb Taylor Collection practicably available to all.

No apology is made for sticking to a successful formula and this book follows the pattern of the first. What makes it intrinsically different is the range of images available from the Taylor Collection. Whilst Robert Burnard tended to favour the southern and eastern parts of the moor, the Taylor's looked largely to the north and west. Also, while Burnard's collection is relatively small, numbering around 500 images dating c.1880–1910, the Taylor Collection comprises almost six times that number, although not all their images are of Dartmoor.

This simple image of Cadover Cross is a striking example of the importance of photographs such as those in the Taylor Collection. Cadover Cross today stands on a shaft well over seven feet in height, one of several such restorations if local accounts are to be believed. William Crossing relates that the broken top of the cross was discovered by soldiers on manoeuvres in 1873, and it was set up by them. When he again saw the cross, in 1901, he described it as being 'thrown down' by cattle. From other photographs we know that by the mid 1920s it was restored to a condition much as we find it today. Thus, where important historic artefacts are subject to change and to damage, photographs such as this provide essential evidence of their earlier condition.

(Tay123a)

Following chapters look in detail at both the modern techniques and benefits of scanning images and at the legacy which three generations of the Taylor family have left to us. It is enough to say here that most of the photographs included in this book have never before appeared in print and for this reason alone I am particularly pleased to have been given the opportunity to work with the Dartmoor National Park and the Dartmoor Trust on this worthy project. Needless to say the musings on the images reflect my own thoughts.

Simon Butler
Manaton, January 2001

The Dartmoor Trust

PHOTOGRAPHY AND THE DARTMOOR ARCHIVE

At the time this book goes to press the Dartmoor Trust continues to pursue its objective of establishing an archive for Dartmoor that will provide for students, researchers, and those with an interest in the moor a single point of call for many of their needs. Though not confined to photography the Trust recognises the importance of collecting and storing photographic images, not least because so many early pictures are in danger of being lost, along with the information relating to them. This particular interest in printed and photographic images springs from the current debate on aspects of photographic storage and retrieval brought about by new technology which, for the first time, allows images to be copied cheaply and effectively in large numbers without the need for expert conservation techniques, spacious storage facilities in temperature controlled environments, and complex card indexing. Computers and dedicated software allow the digital storage of each image and information relating to it that can be instantly accessed from disk or via the internet. Quantity poses few problems and several hundred images can be stored on a single CD, copies of which can easily be made.

The earlier book *Dartmoor Century* contained a chapter on how the Dartmoor Trust was established as a charitable body, outlining its aims and aspirations. These extend far beyond the founding of an archive for Dartmoor which in reality comprises only a small part of the Trust's business, although recently it has increasingly exercised the talents of its individual members all of whom give their time freely and enthusiastically to the Trust's work.

As part of its investigation into the Dartmoor Archive the Dartmoor Trust has quite properly sought advice and co-operation from a wide range of sources, first to establish the need for such an archive, and also to ensure that current practices in professional archiving were understood and followed. Clearly there was a need also to ensure that the Dartmoor Archive did not simply attempt to replicate what already existed in other archives and record offices. The resulting feasibility study, which has garnered information and advice from sources throughout Devon, and further afield, is the foundation on which the Trust aims to raise funding for Dartmoor's own archive.

One of the facts emerging from this study into contemporary photographic archiving was how few protocols have been agreed or established. Indeed those working with the Trust often found themselves somewhat further down the road than those from whom advice was being sought. This is no

The Dartmoor Trust was formed in 1996 after the Dartmoor National Park Authority received a substantial bequest from a former lady resident of the moor. The bequest stipulated that the money be used for the good of Dartmoor. After much deliberation and consultation it was proposed that a charitable trust be set up, not only to make the best use of the original bequest, but to attract further donations, and by doing so to expand the work of the Trust.

The Dartmoor Trust logo is based upon the earliest known example of a silver penny which was minted at Lydford, Devon c.AD 973-5. It shows the head of King Edgar (944-975), younger son of King Edmund.

reflection upon those professionals engaged in this area of research but rather is an indication of how rapid developments in the available technology keep the goal posts (if they ever existed in this field!) constantly on the move.

The Getty Museum in California is among the world's foremost institutions in photographic conservation. Its magnificent new hilltop site overlooking Los Angeles and the Pacific coast contains superb offices, studios and archive facilities specifically designed to house their unparalleled photography collection. But even with this wonderful resource it was clear from a visit to the museum that the expertise held by those working with the Dartmoor Trust in the matter of digital storage and retrieval of images was at the cutting edge as far as current practice was concerned. What is important therefore is that the Dartmoor Archive establishes, as far as its work with photographs is concerned, working methods and protocols that are flexible enough to absorb advances in the technology whilst sharing and incorporating best practice established by others. As so often with the world of computer technology if you wait for the hard- and software capable of providing the perfect solution, you wait in vain.

And time is of the essence. While photographs themselves are lost through deterioration, or are simply discarded, as important is the loss of those who can identify the images and the people, places and events they portray. This is particularly evident through the production of the Community History Series, also published by Halsgrove. These works often include several hundred photographs collected from within communities, mostly from individual family albums. In order to obtain information about the image it is usually to an elderly resident that authors turn for information; with the passing years, such opportunities are all too fleeting.

The importance of linking image with information is vital and is one of the counters to the suggestion that existing archives can manage quite well without a Dartmoor Archive intruding upon their territory. By placing the archive firmly within the locale this aspect of information-gathering at least becomes more feasible and more likely to occur.

By concentrating initially on photography in their bid for funding, the Dartmoor Trust looks to work methodically towards the eventual establishment of an all-encompassing archive. This is a first step. While there is still some way to go and funding yet to find, the aim of founding an archive for Dartmoor will proceed, if only because necessity dictates.

Digital Images

SCANNING, STORING AND RESTORATION

Photography is a chemical process which early practitioners saw as an important step in combining the traditions of art with the disciplines of science. It is no coincidence that pioneers of photography made much of the exactitude with which a photograph could duplicate an image from nature, whether it be a delicate frond of bracken or a landscape. In 1835 William Henry Fox Talbot captured a tiny image of a window at Laycock Abbey thus creating the first photographic negative from which, in theory, an infinite number of positive copies might be made. Five years later he announced his invention to the world and thus photography was born.

In later years photography was to develop its own genres, moving away from concepts which saw it imitating art, echoing the traditions of portraiture, still lifes and landscapes. Most obvious of these new directions was documentary photography in which the camera was used to record the world around it, often for no other reason than it was recognised that the world was facing increasingly rapid change. For the first time it was possible to show exactly how things looked, and thus accurately to measure change through time. It is principally this kind of image with which this book is concerned.

'How things looked...' This untitled image, one of the stereograph images in the Taylor Collection, shows a cottager and his family at the door of their simple thatched dwelling, believed to be in Sampford Spiney. The photograph dates from the mid 1890s. The two little boys dressed in knicker-bockers and gaiters shade their eyes from the sun and appear somewhat camera shy. The old lady at her spinning wheel wears a lace cap and lace-edged apron (Dartmoor cottagers were employed by the lacemakers of Honiton - part of Queen Victoria's mourning apparel was made here) and behind her stands an elderly bearded gent smoking a pipe. A sheep stands partly hidden by the wheel.

(Robin Fenner)

Where is Dartmoor's oldest photograph?

The answer to this will never be known of course, but in any attempt at archiving photographs such a question is bound to be asked. In the earlier volume, *Dartmoor Century*, a Devon photograph was included believed to have been taken by Talbot himself, showing the defences at Plymouth Citadel and dated 1857. Some of Robert Burnard's photographs, on which that first book was based, date from the early 1890s and it was from around this time that popular photography reached the moor.

Crossing a Dartmoor stream – another stereograph image from the Taylor Collection. Such pictures were popular from the mid 1850s through to the early twentieth century. A pair of photographic images was fixed on to a single card (in this instance measuring 100x165mm) and viewed through a stereoscope which thus appeared to the viewer to be three dimensional. The photographs themselves were not identical having been taken on a dual-lens camera, in effect duplicating the way in which the human eye views objects. Note the dress – fashionable middle class attire for an outing to the country.

(Robin Fenner)

One of the earliest photographs from the Burnard collection, dated 1887. The original albums of this superb collection, which was the subject of the first Dartmoor Century book and exhibition, are now held by the Dartmoor Trust.

(courtesy of the Sayer family)

16

Perhaps the earliest depiction of photography in Devon? Peter Orlando Hutchinson's water-colour entitled 'The Granary at Sand in the Parish of Sidbury, Devon - sketched on the spot, July 31 1851' shows a number of gentlemen discussing the old building behind them. In the right foreground is a camera, possibly one belonging to Hutchinson's friend Nicholas Heineken whose many interests included music, invention, and photography. He was also a member of the Devonshire Association. The little boy and the dog looking on reflect a typical touch of Hutchinson humour.

A number of references to early photography in Devon appear in Jeremy Butler's book Travels in Victorian Devon, *based on the life of Hutchinson, who also took an interest in photography. Though he visited Dartmoor with his sketchbook no known photographs exist.*

(courtesy Devon Record Office)

The earliest pictorial reference this author has found relating to photography in the county dates from 1851 and appears as a watercolour in Jeremy Butler's recently published work *Travels in Victorian Devon* (Halsgrove, 2000). It shows a party of men standing outside a barn in east Devon. A camera stands on a tripod behind them. The book contains earlier reference to the photographer, a Mr Heineken, who was out and about in the Devon countryside three years or so before the founding of the Royal Photographic Society in London, in 1853. We have no evidence that he came to Dartmoor. Somewhere out there is Dartmoor's earliest datable photograph, waiting to be discovered.

Being negative and positive

Early photographers found that the use of a square glass plate which had been treated with light-sensitive chemicals provided a convenient and cost-efficient method by which to create their negatives. Experimentation with different materials and different chemicals was part of the fun of discovery, but by the 1860s most photographers had settled for the use of glass plates. The chemical treatment of the surface of the plate was developed commercially to the point at which a photographer could purchase them ready for use, rather than laboriously preparing them in the darkroom. These provided a consistency of image and reliable exposure times, and they were to remain in use up to and after the invention of celluloid film which was cheaper, lighter and less prone to accidental damage.

Glass plate negatives are fragile and a number in the Taylor Collection have been broken, such as this one showing Cole's Dartmoor Inn at Sherwell, Plymouth. The top image is clearly damaged and is reproduced in its original condition. The lower image has been enhanced digitally and repaired. Although all images in the digitised collection are copied in their original state these pictures indicate the value of digital technology for the ease with which such improvements can be made.
(TayP3312)

The general use of glass plates up until the early decades of the twentieth century has ensured that many photographs taken using this medium have failed to survive. The author was told by the grandson of an early North Devon marine photographer that, as a boy, he and his brother stood on a beach near Northam skipping glass plate negatives out across the waves as 'Mother, didn't want they cluttering up the house.' Anyone faced with the sheer weight of a box of glass plates will have some appreciation of 'Mother's' dilemma. How many thousands of photographs have been destroyed can never be reckoned and only in relatively recent times have glass plate negatives been appreciated for their historic worth – almost irrespective of their subject.

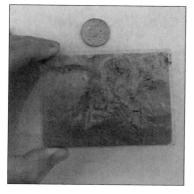

Of the 3500 images in the Taylor Collection, approximately one-quarter are on glass plates, the remainder on film. Ironically it is the older glass plates which today are the least in danger of decay for, kept in reasonable conditions, they are inherently more stable than the later film negatives, the latter being more subject to fading if exposed to daylight and to chemical deterioration. Of course dropping a box of glass plates is not recommended. Such collections are irreplaceable and, even in the most secure hands, the making available of original images exposes them to damage or loss. The digitisation of all such images allows the originals to be stored safely and permanently while enabling access to the copied versions in a multitude of formats depending upon how they are to be used. Moreover in the scanning process itself the original image can be restored and enhanced where necessary, although in no instance have the images in the Taylor Collection been 'retouched' in any way during the digital processing.

The basis of digital capture of photographic images

There is no doubt that the future of archiving and storage of photographic images, along with documents and prints, lies in digitisation, i.e. the capture of pictures and text as binary data. In most commercial media applications it is in this form in which information is transferred from one source to another, or from one medium to another. This book for instance was entirely produced in digital form up to the point at which it was printed.

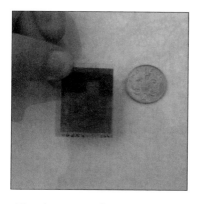

The three main formats of transparency comprising the Taylor Collection (shown for scale against a 2p piece). Top: a glass plate negative (80x105mm approx), centre: a medium format celluloid film negative (90x60mm approx.), and a standard format film negative (30x40mm approx.). Care is essential in handling fragile glass plates, whilst the film negatives can cause problems during scanning as they tend not to lie flat on the scanner bed.

It is worth noting that commercial organisations, especially in the media world, are likely to use AppleMacintosh computers rather than PCs as the software for these machines, particularly powerful applications relating to the creation and manipulation of images, is dedicated to such use. AppleMacs are also configured for the use of cross-platform applications (ie the transfer or manipulation of data between different systems). The heated debate between PC/Apple users on the merits of their respective computers continues, but the fact of the matter is that both types can be successfully used for digital capture of images.

To transfer an image from its original form (in the case of the Taylor Collection from a negative) into a digitised file it is necessary to place the image on a scanner attached to a computer. These days even the most mundane of home PCs come with a scanner attached and these are, by and

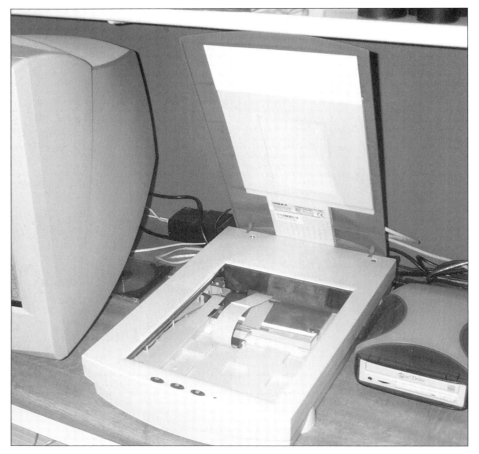

A typical domestic flatbed scanner, in this case a Umax Astra, attached to an AppleMacintosh computer. The transparency scanning attachment is visible in the raised hood, this providing a second light source. On the right is a CD burner – useful if quantities of images are to be scanned and transferred to CD – the primary storage medium used for the Taylor Collection.

large, perfectly adequate for the digital capture of both mono and colour images for archive purposes. High resolution scanners are required for colour images for output to print, the cost of these putting them well beyond the pocket of most users – although domestic scanners can transfer colour images successfully to mono format for archiving and print.

For scanning transparencies special attachments to the ordinary scanner are required. These take a number of forms ranging from a simple and cheap prismatic device to a dedicated scanning hood in which the lid of scanner contains a second light source. For quality this latter version is recommended. Small scanning devices dedicated to transparencies are available but these usually accommodate only 35mm negatives or slides.

During the scanning process the image is copied from its original form and is held as an electronic file on the computer. In this state it can be viewed on the computer screen and manipulated in a number of ways. For example, the Taylor Collection images would initially appear in their original negative form, often making it difficult to discern just what the photograph shows. Once digitised the picture can be changed instantly to a positive image. Indeed, one of the fascinations of working on such collections is to see the pictures being transformed in this way – often revealing them as 'real' pictures for the first time since they were taken.

Each photograph can also be enhanced, increasing or decreasing contrast, lightening or darkening the picture in order to create the best possible image.

Left: *The impressive size of the J. Taylor & Sons Union Leather Works, Flora Street, Plymouth, located close to the railway, indicates the standing of the company within the city.* Below: *The Union Works shop front decorated for the Western Evening Herald's* Shopping Week *in 1935 (for which it won first prize).* Bottom left: *Frank Taylor stopping for lunch in the Plym Valley, 1915 (taken from a lantern slide).* Bottom right: *Sydney Taylor Snr, 1915.*

(Tay3475, Tay35135, Tay13gs and Robin Fenner)

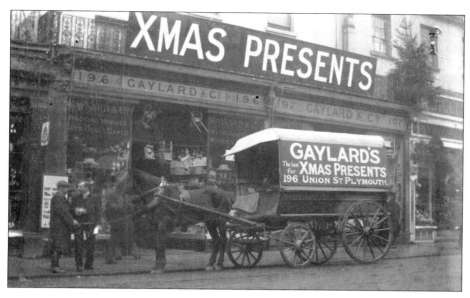

Gaylards store in Union Street,
Plymouth, December 1914.
Sydney Taylor Snr, who ran the
business, can be seen next to
the man holding the horse.

(Tay1492b)

Frank's brother, Sydney Taylor Snr (1868-1946) pursued an amateur interest in photography for much of his life although his major contribution to the photography of Dartmoor was through his son, Sydney Jnr. Even so, Sydney Snr was a close friend of many of the great names associated with the moor including R. Hansford Worth, William Crossing and Eden Phillpotts.

An advertisement for Gaylards toy store, one of the 36 lantern slides in the Taylor Collection.

(Tay16gs)

Sydney Snr married Sophie Ledden in 1896 and they produced two sons, Sydney and Leslie Gaylard. Sydney Snr would be perhaps best known by older Plymouthians for his part in relaunching and running the large toy and stationery retailers, Gaylards, at 196 Union Street, Plymouth, in the 1880s. There are a number of photographs in the collection relating to the Gaylard business which survived until the Second World War when the store was destroyed during a blitz on Plymouth.

Father and son, Sydney Taylor Snr and Jnr crossing the River Erme, 1915.

(Tay 27gs)

Part of a page from the Plymouth Photographic Society 'circulating portfolio' through which members submitted photographs for appraisal and comment. This example concerns the picture of Lew Mill which appears as the first in The Photographs section in this book and which Sydney Jnr had submitted in 1915 as a twenty year old. Eight other comments are as critical as the one shown and, in truth, Taylor's photography was seldom to rise above the level of 'workmanlike'. His strength was in his documentary style, his eye largely taken by details within the landscape. (Robin Fenner)

Marjorie, wife of Sydney Jnr, in the sidecar of the motorcycle on which the couple took regular trips on to the moor.

(Taymisc 84)

Sydney Taylor Jnr (1894-1991) was born in Plymouth, son of Sydney Taylor Snr and nephew to Frank Taylor. It was to the latter that the young Sydney became most closely allied. His daughter, Shirley, recalled that uncle and nephew were inseparable in their dual interests of photography and Dartmoor. Most weekends saw the pair setting out to walk the moor in all weathers, working specific areas in order to compile a year-by-year study of Dartmoor and its people. Their various modes of transport to and from the moor are recorded in some of their photographs, ranging from a motorbike and sidecar to a variety of cars, the latter reflecting a comfortable middle-class lifestyle.

Sydney Jnr became a family partner in the firm of Gaylards until the destruction of its premises by the Luftwaffe, and afterwards joined his uncle Frank at

R. Hansford Worth is among the forerunners of modern archaeological study on Dartmoor and his letter to Sydney Taylor and the accompanying photograph (taken in 1934 at Worth's Fernworthy excavation) confirm the importance of photographic recording of such sites.

(Taymisc 34116 and Robin Fenner)

17 August, 1934.

Dear Mr. Taylor,

My best thanks for your letter, I am delighted to hear that there will be a party from Plymouth to see the circles. I have only been here two days, but the first circle is opening up in a very interesting manner. They are all unusually fine in structure. To my sorrow this particular circle which I am now working on has been disturbed long since by someone who dug a deep pit near the centre, I hope he did not too greatly damage the floor. Apart from that it is excellent.

If you tell your members who come in cars of their own to make their way to the Torquay waterworks intake at Fernworthy on the South Teign they can not miss the circles, but must see us at work on the hills above. Tell them also to bring their lunch, there are no local resources for them - and their teas also if they would like to stay until we drop work at five o'clock.

I am seeing Mr. Jack Rice tomorrow, and I will give him all necessary instructions as to route etc, although he and his drivers are very way-wise. Bring your cameras, I will have at least one circle swept and cleared so that details of structure shall be clearly seen.

With our kindest regards to yourself and Mrs. Taylor, and a hint to our members to make an effort to come,

Yours sincerely,

R. Hansford Worth

A display of Sydney Taylor's cameras, photographic material and books, taken at his home in 1971 when he was in his late seventies. Many of his cameras were later sold at auction by Robin Fenner in 1989.

(Tay7111b)

the Union Leather Works. Theirs was evidently a very happy relationship and Frank is remembered as saying that he 'had found a kindred spirit in his nephew'. They were both active members of the Plymouth Photographic Society.

As Sydney's interest and knowledge of Dartmoor grew so he joined the Dartmoor Preservation Society (which his photographic forebear Robert Burnard had helped to found), and the Devonshire Association. He became closely acquainted with the grande dame of the DPA, Sylvia Sayer (Burnard's grand-daughter), and with many other of the major Dartmoor figures of the day including Eden Phillpotts and R. Hansford Worth.

As a photographer Sydney's output was decidedly documentary in content and style, and few of his pictures are arresting from an artistic viewpoint. Robin Fenner's own analysis of his skills are worth recording here.

Shirley, Sydney Taylor's daughter.

(Tay34gs)

Sydney Taylor was never a highly competent or even accomplished photographer. His value to the world of photography is in his undoubted output. Prolific he most certainly was. He was however more of a 'point and shoot' cameraman as we understand photography today, rather than one whose work may be viewed in terms of the artistic.
He was bent on recording every facet of life on what he called 'God's Acre'. He captured the changing moods of the moor and its seasons, its historical monuments, footpaths, rivers, streams, bridges, architecture, industry and natural history, and certainly in greater depth than any had done either before or since.

Although some of the Taylors' work appeared as postcards and greeting cards, and selected work was created in stereograph format by William Heath, many of the images which now comprise the Taylor Collection have

never been previously published. While dates on the negatives in the Taylor Collection provide clues, it is impossible to define exactly which images were taken by whom, but it is clear that the vast majority come from the lens of Sydney Jnr – and it is due to his perception and diligence that the collection remains intact for our pleasure and interest today.

Along with Dartmoor, his passion was for trains and all things railway, and many of the photographs in the collection represent this abiding interest. As far as Dartmoor is concerned this is a great bonus, for the collection spans the period which saw the demise of railways on and around the moor. His images of the dismantling of the railway line to Princetown are of particular importance.

Sydney married Marjorie Kate Roper in 1922 and the pair had one daughter, Shirley, who appears in many of the family photographs held in the collection. After a long and active life centred in Devon, and on Dartmoor in particular, the family moved to South Africa, where Sydney died in May 1991.

And the Taylor legacy persists to this day. The son of Sydney Jnr's brother, Leslie Gaylard Taylor, is a contemporary photographer, now living in Gloucestershire. And so Brian Taylor is the latest participant in a family tradition lasting well over a hundred years.

One of the many photographs which Taylor devoted to his passion for trains and railways. Here the Princetown railway is shown in its last throes, with rails being lifted at Yennadon for removal following the closure of the line in March 1956.

(Tay7111b)

The Photographs

The Menhir, Lew Mill

Lewtrenchard, 1914. Tay1438

This is the photograph which the twenty-year-old Sydney Taylor Jnr submitted for scrutiny by his fellow members of the Plymouth Photographic Society in 1915. In their criticism of the photograph most complained, justifiably, that central subject, the menhir, was lost against the background. Today of course the composition of the picture is of less importance to the viewer than the changes which it shows.

Robert Burnard relates the discovery of the menhir in his book *Dartmoor Pictorial Records* (1893):

> In 1879 a long stone of granite was discovered, which formed a portion of one of the sides of a leat supplying water to Lew Mill. This attracted the attention of the Rev. S. Baring-Gould, and subsequently the late Rev. W. C. Lukis examined the stone, and it was then found that it was a prehistoric menhir, which had evidently at some period stood erect.
> The stone had been rudely tooled, so as to smooth the edges or angles, except for the lower eighteen inches or two feet, which portion was left in the rough, and formed the earth-fastening part of the menhir. The extreme width of the stone is two feet; at the ground line it is one foot eight inches; above that it bulges out, but contracts at the top to one foot two and a half inches. The height above the ground line is ten feet ten inches.

The Menhir, Lew Mill

Lewtrenchard, November 2000. (Bryan Harper)

Despite the difference in time of almost eighty years these two photographs show remarkably little change. The menhir remains in place although the mound on which it stands is less pronounced. The dwelling itself, although without its coat of white paint is almost unchanged – the chimney stack now has rendering over the brickwork and gone is the smart fence, as are the rose bushes. Most immediately apparent is the absence of the trees which once formed such an effective backdrop to the scene.

Robert Burnard's photograph, taken on 13 May 1893, depicts the menhir just a few years after it was found and re-erected by Sabine Baring-Gould. It shows the barns and cottage (with washing on the line) that stood to the left of the house shown in the main photographs

(Burnard Collection)

The small building to the right of the menhir also remains much the same, although the chimney stack in the earlier picture is now missing.

Belstone Manor Pound

Belstone Parish, 1934. Tay3412

W. G. Hoskins in his book *Devon* describes Belstone in an unkindly way, remarking on the blight of new building in the village since it was 'discovered'. Hoskins was writing in the 1950s and Belstone today is attractive to those wishing to live in a rural location and yet have access to good transport links. Its proximity to the A30, Dartmoor's northern bypass (a highway exciting great opposition from conservation groups when it was proposed), ensures its popularity.

There are many types of pound on the moor. Those best known are the prehistoric enclosures which served a variety purposes including the enfolding of sheep and cattle. Drift pounds, from a later historical period, held animals that were found straying or were illegally depastured within the Forest of Dartmoor – and which would be released only on payment of a fine. Manor pounds, of which that at Belstone is one of many to survive (and even larger numbers are recalled in field and placenames), served local communities in much the same way.

Belstone Manor Pound

Belstone Parish, October 2000. (Bryan Harper)

The pound cottage is instantly recognisable and except for the missing chimney stack is largely unchanged. The old wooden sash windows have given way to double-glazed units, a practical if not always stylish answer to harsh winters. The corrugated iron shed has gone as have the other outbuildings, although the telephone pole (now becoming a rarer sight) remains.

Note the trees: ubiquitous evergreens that forever seem out of place wherever they proliferate on the moor.

The pound wall has seen some renovation since 1934, particularly to the left of the gateway, a sign that such features are increasingly recognised as worthy of care. Over the years more than one gate would have come and gone – and the present one will soon need some attention.

The notice reads 'Belstone Pound. This was originally used to pound stray animals until claimed by their owners. It is now a garden to be enjoyed by all.'

(Bryan Harper)

Lower Cherry Brook Bridge
Cherry Brook Bridge c.1920. Taymisc.94

A photograph of this old turnpike bridge, taken by Robert Burnard in 1887, appears in the first volume of *Dartmoor Century.* This Taylor photograph, taken around thirty years later, reveals few changes during that time.

Sydney Taylor's motorbike and sidecar stands on the road to the left of the bridge. The photographer favoured this type of transport, as did many others in the 1920s and 30s, as a popular alternative to the more expensive car.

The Dartmoor ponies have the appearance of being larger than those animals typically held on the moor today, while the river, seen here in the summer months, wanders naturally between the reedy banks.

Longaford Tor is the landmark in the distance.

Sydney Taylor on his Royal Enfield combination, 1920 – somewhere on Dartmoor. Note the fledgling conifer plantation in the background.

(Taymisc.98)

Lower Cherry Brook Bridge
Cherry Brook Bridge, November 2000. (Bryan Harper)

The autumn and winter of the year 2000 will be remembered on Dartmoor as being one of the wettest on record. With the land saturated, each new cloudburst saw river levels quickly rising leading to waterlogged fields and flooded roads. Towns and villages at the edge of the moor caught the full fury of the floodwaters as they cascaded off the moor, and many homes were flooded time and again. Bridges too suffered, with parapets washed away, eroded banks leading to partial collapse.

This photograph, taken on one of the few dry days in November 2000, shows the river is contained well within its banks. The gates across the arches (preventing the passage of livestock under the bridge) are intact despite earlier spates. On closer inspection the banks reveal that a great deal of reconstruction has gone on, aiding the free passage of the river along this stretch. The Dartmoor National Park Authority has participated in similar work on a number of rivers where banks are at threat, either through flood damage or by erosion due to public access.

The parapet on the bridge has been heightened and the roadsides built up. The structure of the bridge has been braced by steel tie-bars through its width.

Haytor from the West
Ilsington Parish, 1967. Tay6711b

Haytor's original name 'High Tor' is appropriate for although it is nowhere near the highest point on the moor (457 metres against Yes Tor's 619) it is the most singular in size and shape, and of course among the most accessible. William Crossing in his *Guide to Dartmoor* refers to a mistaken identity made by an earlier writer:

> *The moormen, in accordance with their habit of duplicating the final syllable when naming the tors, usually speak of it as 'Heyter Tar', and as 'Heyter Rocks', and this seems to have misled the writer of a brief account of the moor published many years ago. He calls it Athur Tor, or Solar Tor, deriving, we suppose, the latter name from the former, and evidently regarding it as a place where sacrifices were once offered to the sun god.*

Smile as we may at this, passing Haytor on a hot summer's afternoon one might easily be led to believe that all the world's sun-worshippers had gathered there to witness an imminent solar event.

Haytor from the West
Ilsington Parish, November, 2000. (Bryan Harper)

At first sight these two views appear to be identical, except of course for the walkers in the more recent picture. But they provide a clue to major changes that have taken place in thirty years. Compare the ground on the right hand side of the pictures. The worn turf in the recent picture provides stark evidence of the effect of millions of feet on popular sites such as Haytor. Here, the natural routes up to the Tor from the car parks below appear as permanent scars upon the landscape.

And such erosion is by no means confined to the summer months when visitor numbers are at their height. The wet winter of 2000–2001 necessitated an advisory restriction of access to some of the more frequented footpaths such was the severity of erosion. This is just one of the problems faced by the Dartmoor National Park Authority; balancing visitor numbers against conservation needs.

Haytor Granite Tramway
Ilsington Parish, 1967.   Tay677a

Five quarries were worked in the Haytor area during the nineteenth century and supplied building stone for many grand projects, famously for major buildings in London, including London Bridge in 1825. In the eighteenth century James Templer of Stover had developed the ball clay industry in the Bovey Basin and constructed a canal originally planned to run from Teignmouth to Bovey Tracey, although only part was completed.   George Templer inherited his father's estate and planned a link from the quarries at Haytor to the canal using a granite tramway. Wagons, the wheels of which fitted over the flanged granite 'rails', were drawn by teams of horses over the 8.5 miles down to the canal at Teigngrace.

This early view of the quarries at Haytor gives an indication of the size and extent of the operations in the mid-nineteenth century.

Haytor Granite Tramway
Ilsington Parish, January 2001.   (Bryan Harper)

Although the route of the tramway can still be followed with ease across Haytor Down, this photograph shows that in thirty years turf has grown over the granite, partly obscuring the surface of the rails.

With sidings and branches taken into account it is estimated that there were 10 miles of track in all.   Where the branchlines met the main tramway granite points systems were operated.   Holes drilled in some of the stones at these junctions indicate a hinged guide arrangement which sent trucks down the appropriate track.

Prowses Crossing, Dousland
Walkhampton Parish, 1957. Tay578b

The GWR railway journey from Plymouth to Princetown was considered to offer one of the great delights of branchline travel in Britain, meandering as it did through wonderful scenery, ever rising to the heights of Dartmoor. Yelverton was the junction for the forward journey to Princetown, and Dousland station was the stop following. After Dousland the line crossed a little road that joined the B3212 near the Burrator Inn, and shortly after crossed a lane at Prowses Crossing.

The picture shows the old GWR style crossing gates in place in 1957, a year or so after the line ceased operation.

Another view of Prowses Crossing in 1957, showing the wicket gate by which means the line could be crossed when the level crossing gate itself was closed.

(Tay578a)

'The Crossing', Dousland
Walkhampton Parish, December 2000. (Bryan Harper)

The original trackbed is still discernable and now forms the driveway into 'The Crossing', a private dwelling, formerly the crossing keeper's cottage. The building is much altered and extended. Here the current owner, Mrs Duffy, stands close to where the Princetown train used to steam its way to and from the moor.

A postcard copied by Sydney Taylor and captioned 'The Princetown Express'. Note the line is heavily fenced against the encroachment of livestock.

(TayP718)

Rock Hotel, Yelverton
Yelverton, 1913. Tay1375

In his book *Dartmoor Inns* (Devon Books, 1992) author Tom Quick provides a concise account of the origins of this building:

The Rock Inn is one of the oldest buildings in Yelverton. Records show it to have been in existence in 1828 as a dwelling-house known as Rock House. It is thought originally it was a farmhouse dating from the 15th century and the structure of the nearby stables has been estimated to date from that period.

Records of 1862 show William Shillabeer, Victualler, Rock Hotel, but how long before that it became an hotel is uncertain. For a while, it was known as the Blatchford Rock Hotel. The hotel had been developed with the acquisition of the old stables from Sir Massey Lopes by the Shillabeer sisters, who in 1905 were joined by Algy Langton, their nephew. In 1966 the hotel closed and parts of it were made into flats. The bars that occupied the main section of the premises remained and became the Rock Inn.

The photograph at the foot of the page is one of a number of copied images that appear in the Taylor Collection. It appears to date from around 1870 and from the placement of the figures in formal pose (a number of them in uniform) there is an air of a special event taking place. Perhaps someone is moving in, or out, or is the post box on the right a possible object of attention? The picture is full of interesting detail, not least in how the main building differs from that shown in the 1913 photograph. But note also the white building on the left with the arched windows and the pigeon holes near the roof line. The smart wagonette on the left bears the name of Groom & Co, a photographer from Union Street in Plymouth. Groom was a friend of John, the first in the Taylor family to take up photography.

Rock Inn, Yelverton
Yelverton, November 2000. (Bryan Harper)

In the contemporary photograph the central body of the original hotel building can still be discerned. When compared, these three photographs throw a fascinating light on the changes that have occurred in 130 years or so.

Grimstone & Sortridge Leat, Plaster Down
Whitchurch Parish, c.1920. TayWB28

Dartmoor has many miles of leat, channelled waterways through which water is carried by gravity to a point of use. Some of these, such as the Plymouth, or Drake's, Leat, which dates from Elizabethan times, are of historical interest, and others, such as Devonport Leat demonstrate the engineering skills of the eighteenth century. Many leats are in use today, particularly for bringing water to farms, and because they are thus part of Dartmoor's 'living heritage', they are not protected as are other antiquities. Alas the care with which many were built is not carried through to modern times, with some landowners simply breaking into an existing leat wall in order to channel water elsewhere.

The Grimstone & Sortridge Leat is in fact a series of interconnected channels taking water from the River Walkham to a number of holdings in the area.

Grimstone & Sortridge Leat, Plaster Down
Whitchurch Parish, November 2000. (Bryan Harper)

As the provision of piped water becomes ubiquitous, so these man-made waterways are in danger of falling into decay. Here the channel is less well-defined than in the earlier picture and the banks are broken down by cattle and ponies.

The road runs across a clapper bridge (unmetalled in the earlier photograph) which has been strengthened by the placement of two concrete pipes, with the original granite parapet placed atop.

The birch wood in the right middle distance has disappeared.

In 1943 Plaster (or Plaister) Down was the site chosen for the establishment of an American military hospital and, following the Normandy invasion, thousands of wounded men were shipped back to be treated here. After the war the huge complex of buildings, including a cinema, was used to house Polish and German prisoners of war before repatriation. Its last use was to temporarily house Ugandan refugees fleeing from the excesses of their President, Idi Amin, in 1972. Four years later the camp was demolished and now almost no trace remains.

Bedford Square, Tavistock
Tavistock, c.1895. TayBB38

This photograph of the centre of Tavistock, taken towards the end of the Victorian era, contains many details of note. Mining, which had made the town rich, by this time had subsided and the population too had shrunk from 9000 to around 6000. From Bedford Square a new road west was built towards Plymouth and Drake Road (seen running up from the Square, centre) providing access to the new station serving a second rail link to the town. The railway viaduct can be glimpsed through the trees while the telegraph poles next to the station stand out on the horizon. To the left of Drake Road are the offices of the *Tavistock Gazette*, then published by Thomas Greenfield who also ran a stockbroking and bookselling business. To the right is Bedford House, premises of Yelland & Co.

The presence of horse-drawn traffic is amply evident. Note also the drain cover in the gutter on the left, replicated by the modern cover in the contemporary photograph.

Workmen installing new sewers in the shadow of the Viaduct, Tavistock c.1900.

(TayBB70)

Bedford Square, Tavistock
Tavistock, November 2000. (Bryan Harper)

Details of the Victorian town are echoed everywhere in this photograph despite all the modern trappings. The Town Hall, the Duke of Bedford's statue behind the granite posts on the right, all remain, as do so many smaller features throughout the two scenes. We are reminded however just how much we have become slaves to the car, and the intrusion of traffic signs, the pedestrian crossing, road markings and bollards all detract from the view.

Fitzford, Tavistock

Tavistock, c.1895. TayBB21

This scene contains two significant features of the town, Fitzford Church (St Mary Magdalene) and the town gas works, both of which have interesting histories. The church was designed and built by Henry Clutton in 1856-7 under the hand of the Duke of Bedford whose aim was to provide a 'chapel of ease' for those in the surrounding suburbs. Pevsner in *Buildings of England: Devon* describes it as successfully combining Romanesque and Transitional Gothic styles – and remarks on the detached campanile-like tower. In fact the church was to undergo a major transition, of faith not design, in 1952, when (after it had remained unused for some time), it transferred from the Church of England use to Roman Catholicism.

The gas works (seen on the left) were the brainchild of John Rundle, a businessman and ironmaster, who was determined to bring the benefits of gas lighting to the town. The gas company was founded in 1831 and buildings sprang up in a field at the foot of the Callington Road. Gas Works Lane (now Maudlin's Lane) ran alongside the new works. In 1906 a new gas works was built near West Bridge.

Note the smoke from all the woodfires in the town.

Fitzford, Tavistock

Tavistock, December 2000. (Bryan Harper)

New housing has spread along the roads out of the town centre, hidden by the shrubbery on the left. Three or four post-war houses nestle up against the church the outward appearance of which is almost completely unchanged.

Gone are the gas works – cause of a fire in the Weslyan Chapel in Barley Market Street, in 1834, the resultant panic leading to two deaths among the congregation, and a number of injured.

A view over Tavistock towards the viaduct c.1900.

(TayBB22)

Deancombe Farm, Burrator

Sheepstor Parish, 1935. Tay35127

One of several 'ghost' farms in the catchment area of Burrator Reservoir, a number of which were finally abandoned in the 1920s. Deancombe's ruins now, as Hemery relates in *High Dartmoor*, take on a 'nostalgic and emancipated significance', although when first describing the site, in 1965, he recalls his shock at finding 'this gaunt, unmellowed ruin with seemingly, the heavy Victorian hand of Massey Lopes upon it.'

The Lopes family were important landowners here and when Sir Ralph Lopes died in 1854 he was succeeded by his son Sir Massey whose influence on his tenants reverberated through later generations. 'ML 1858' carved on a lintel above a stable door recalls the Lopes dynasty. His son became Lord Roborough.

The 'potato cave' near Deancombe Farm.

(John Earle)

William Crossing describes three caches or caves in the vicinity of the farm, one of which the farmer called his 'potato cave'. These, Crossing says, locals ascribed to the concealment of illicit stills, although *he* felt that they were made and used by tinners.

Deancombe Farm, Burrator

Sheepstor Parish, December 2000. (John Earle)

To talk of 'haunted ruins' is to overplay the effect that coming across these abandoned farms, even on the dimpsiest of evenings, can have. However the remains are poignant insofar as they speak of the moor people who once made their living here off the land – a tough existence.

Hemery remarks on the remaining line of granite blocks, the stands on which a rick of hay or straw would be built in order to keep it off the ground. They can still be seen today.

Remains of the rick stand at Deancombe Farm.

(John Earle)

Beetor Cross, North Bovey
North Bovey Parish, 1913. Tay136

In Bill Harrison's manuscript 'Ancient Dartmoor Crosses' (now to be published by Halsgrove/Devon Books), he provides a concise history of this cross, with information gleaned by early writers as to its origin.

Rowe in 1848 called it Bector Cross and described it as standing in a field adjoining the crossroads, and in 1857 Ormerod made a drawing of it acting as a gatepost between two fields on Hele Moor, probably at the same location, and later wrote that in 1871 it was moved to act in the same capacity as a gatepost at a gateway leading out of Hele plantation to Hele House. This was confirmed by Page in 1889 when he referred to 'Bector Cross' being moved about 1871 to serve as a gatepost in the grounds of 'Hill House'.

Crossing, who begged to differ somewhat with the above history, tells us that it was moved to its present position in 1900, probably near to its original position at the crossroads of two major tracks between Moreton/Tavistock and Chagford/Ashburton. This was a spot also known as 'Watching Place', a macabre title, for it is said a gibbet once stood here, the last to be used in the Dartmoor area. Legend has it the cross was erected to commemorate a battle between the Ancient Britons and the Saxons.

Beetor Cross, North Bovey
North Bovey Parish, December 2000. (Bryan Harper)

Harrison records over 130 crosses such as Beetor and covers the known history of each. It is clear that few have withstood intact the rigours of all that time, weather and people, have thrown at them. Many have been moved at one time or another – and who knows what number have been entirely lost. The Taylor Collection contains many photographs of these crosses and as a record of any changes to such monuments they are of considerable interest.

The Dartmoor Trust were fortunate to receive from the estate of the Lady Sylvia Sayer two albums of photographs of crosses, taken in the 1920s and 1930s by George Thompson. These photographs help support written evidence and hearsay of changes over the past eighty years or so, and will be published to support Harrison's book.

Spurrell's Cross before and after restoration, August 1930. It was again restored in 1954 under the auspices of the Dartmoor Preservation Association.

(George Thompson)

Merchant or Marchant's Cross, Meavy
Meavy Parish, c.1937. Taymisc.61

A photograph of this cross was included in the first volume of *Dartmoor Century*. Robert Burnard's photograph showed the cross standing alongside a dilapidated cottage, now a modern dwelling. A brief history of the cross accompanies Burnard's photograph.

This photograph is interesting as it provides visual evidence of Pauline Hemery's story in *The Book of Meavy* (Halsgrove, 1999):

> Up the road and over the cattle grid is Marchant's Cross and Marchant's Cottage. The cross is documented here in 1291 and according to W. G. Hoskins it is 'a roughly hewn monolithic granite cross with short arms inscribed with Latin cross on front and back.' It was knocked down by Mr Jury driving Bill Northmore's car when the brakes failed in the Morris car in 1937.

Not even the lucky black cat (seen here sitting on the hedge) was able to save the cross on this occasion.

Merchant or Marchant's Cross, Meavy
Meavy Parish, January 2001. (Bryan Harper)

Contrary to Hoskins' opinion Burnard described this cross as 'the tallest and best shaped of all the Dartmoor crosses'. Whatever one's view, here is evidence of how even the stoutest of granite shafts is prone to damage and decay. The Taylor Collection records more than one cross serving as a farm gatepost, while how many others may have disappeared over the centuries is a matter for reflection.

Bill Northmore and his little Morris tourer which knocked down Marchant's Cross in 1937.

(Pauline Hemery)

View towards Brent Hill

South Brent Parish, 1940. Tay4070

In his book *Worth's Dartmoor* (David & Charles, 1988), R. Hansford Worth, who appears in Sydney Taylor's photographs of the hut circle excavation at Fernworthy (see page 28), provides an explanation of the origin of Brent Hill's name:

> *Brent: a word barely obsolescent, 'steep, lofty, prominent'. Occurs in Brent Hill, in the parish of South Brent, and in Brent Tor, in the parish of the same name. The most familiar present use of the word is in the phrase, 'brent brow', descriptive of a lofty forehead. Both Brent Hill and Brent Tor are border heights of exceptionally bold outline, and from their abruptness and their height form landmarks visible over wide stretches of country.*

The typical moorland border landscapes, as represented in these photographs, are little studied compared to the high moor, and yet they hold many clues as to earlier settlement on Dartmoor. Echoes of the prehistoric boundaries which extend across the moor are to be discerned in modern field hedges, while lanes are known to follow the ancient trackways that led on and off the moor.

View towards Brent Hill

South Brent Parish, December 2000. (Bryan Harper)

We take for granted views which are familiar to us, and it is an easy mistake to assume that landscapes such as this are 'natural'. In fact, ignoring the geologic mass which dictates the shape of the land, this is wholly a manmade landscape, and one on which the pattern of history is laid.

From the farmstead hidden among the trees, to the hedges and lanes, and to the new tree planting by the Woodland Trust in the foreground, this view has been configured by those who live and work here. Economics have certainly played more of a part than aesthetics. It is a common misconception, held particularly by those whose appreciation of scenery such as this is fleeting, that the countryside is a place best left to nature. But as country traditions are eroded who is to say what this landscape would look like in another century or so?

HM Prison, Dartmoor

Princetown, 1913. Tay1348

Thomas Tyrwhitt, the great 'improver' of Dartmoor, laid the foundation stone of what was to be a war prison on 20 March 1806.   French and American prisoners of war first arrived in 1809 to face the bleak prospect of incarceration in overcrowded and insanitary conditions. At one time 9000 prisoners lived here subject to disease, malnutrition and ill-treatment, which led on occasion to riot. The last of these prisoners left in 1816.

An obvious attraction in later consigning convicts to Dartmoor prison was its remote location and the difficulties facing any prisoner planning escape. There are many tales of half-dead convicts fetching up at remote farms having lost their way on the moor.

This photograph shows some of the many buildings that surrounded the prison's core, within a high stone wall just glimpsed between the buildings in the foreground. In the mid 1840s the British Naptha Company leased part of the prison for the distillation of peat into naptha on a commercial scale. Candles and gas for lighting their premises were among the by-products of this enterprise which lasted only for a few years. The gas holders in the picture reveal that gas was still used for lighting and heating in 1913.

Note the little guard-hut in the field on the left.

HM Prison, Dartmoor

Princetown, February 2001. (Bryan Harper)

A high razor-wire fence now surrounds the prison which, at night, is lit by the sombre yellow of sodium lights – a diffuse glow which it is possible to see for many miles from high points on the moor.

The prison remains as forbidding as ever and despite periodic rumours of its closure it appears to be a permanent fixture. It is also a major source of employment for warders, and others, and remains a magnet for tourists, evidenced by the often crowded carpark which overlooks the prison from the Princetown–Two Bridges road.

The Warren House Inn
Near Postbridge, 1913. Tay1370

This photograph is believed to show Frank Taylor waiting outside the inn door, in 1913. The dog appears to belong to the pub for he appears in an earlier photograph which shows Thomas Hext, the landlord, standing in the porch.

According to Tom Quick in *Dartmoor Inns:*

> *The Warren House Inn was built in 1845 and replaced the New Inn that stood on the opposite side of the road, and which had been demolished that same year. This meant that the inn had moved from common land in the parish of North Bovey to Duchy Land. When it was first built, the Warren House Inn was called The Moreton Inn and it was not until later that century that the name was changed. The reference is to the nearby rabbit warrens, where the tin miners of the locality would keep the rabbits that provided a source of fresh meat.*

The inn's sign, showing three rabbits in a circle, the ears of each touching the ears of the adjacent rabbit, is a tinners' emblem – a study of which is subject of a forthcoming book.

The Warren House Inn
Near Postbridge, December 2000. (Bryan Harper)

There is quite possibly a book of historic photographs to be produced based entirely upon this public house. It has long been a favourite of postcard photographers while over the years countless thousands of holidaymakers have posed here for a snapshot.

The present day building reflects the popularity of the inn as a stopping point for those visiting the moor. Even with its various extensions the bars can become very busy and one can only muse on which other directions the building might possibly expand. The main body of the inn can still easily be traced from its historic and, it has to be said, somewhat more attractive origins.

Thomas Hext, landlord of the Warren House Inn, c.1920.

(Robert Burnard)

Old Cottages, Buckland Monachorum
Buckland Monachorum Parish, 1935. Tay353

This village lies outside the National Park boundaries but in many ways typifies a moorland border village on the western side of Dartmoor. What immediately catches the eye is that the fabric of the building is not granite. The mullioned window in the upper storey adds a touch of refinement and, take away the lean-to beneath it, and the shape of the original house becomes clearer. The walls to the far right are of finer construction while the buttresses on the laneside wall suggest a structural weakness there.

The whole is wonderfully eccentric – a tipsy maiden-aunt of a house in imminent danger of collapse.

'Cruets', Buckland Monachorum
Buckland Monachorum Parish, December 2000. (Bryan Harper)

And collapse it did, to be replaced by the building we see here. The mullioned window survives however – now in the garage wall of 'Cruets', the housename wittily applied by the present owner Mr Salt.

The chimney on the building to the right appears to match that on the older photograph above.

The Taylors had an affection for old buildings and a number of the photographs in their collection capture houses and farms on the verge of ruin. One feels they recognised the importance of recording everyday things which are swept away by time, and only missed when they are gone.

Hele Farm, Buckland Monachorum, scheduled for demolition, 1967.

(Tay6717b)

65

Yelverton

Yelverton, 1913. Tay1376

Originally known as Jump, and a tiny settlement up to the mid 1800s, the guide to *Dartmoor* by Ward Lock & Co, dated 1911, reflects on the rising importance of Yelverton as a centre for touring the moor, emphasizing the rapid growth of such places resulting from easier rail access and the public appetite for holidaying:

> *Although within easy reach of Tavistock, and included within a district regularly traversed by the coaching excursions from that town, Yelverton has attained a position of sufficient importance to claim recognition as a tourist centre in itself. Ten miles distant from Plymouth, it has become practically a suburb of the capital of the West Country, and many of its residents are engaged in business there. It is the nearest genuine moorland stretch, and has gradually become dotted with hotels and lodging houses and with residences, large and small, though it boasts the title of neither village nor town. During the summer it is a favourite resort of visitors, and it has also a growing reputation as a place suited for the residence of consumptives.*

The row of handsome houses and hotels that constitute The Tors at Yelverton are lined alongside the route of the Plymouth & Dartmoor Railway, another enterprise of Sir Thomas Tyrwhitt.

Yelverton

Yelverton, November 2000. (Bryan Harper)

Where cattle once grazed cars now navigate the busy roundabout at the junction where the cross-moorland B3212 leaves the Tavistock–Plymouth road. There are obvious differences to the buildings in the scene yet they retain their air of dignity and charm, as if still waiting for the next Plymouth train to deliver another party of excited holidaymakers.

Granite sleepers from the old P&DR are said now to be used as kerb-stones on the roundabout.

The track of the P&DR is still clearly visible in 1967.

(Tay6712)

Yelverton Station
Yelverton, 1914. Tay1482

Yelverton Station looking towards Plymouth on a snowy day in 1914. The Princetown train steams gently on the left while the train from which the photograph is taken is heading towards Bickleigh and Plymouth. The Plymouth & Dartmoor Railway was opened to Kings Tor in 1823, with the line to Princetown completed by 1825. Used mainly for hauling granite quarried on Dartmoor, the P&DR was never profitable and eventually the southern section only remained, taking clay from Lee Moor. The GWR worked the Yelverton to Princetown line after 1883, and Yelverton Station was built in 1885.

Granite sleepers forming the track of the P&DR photographed near Yelverton, 1934.

(Tay3452)

Six miles as the crow flies, the train from Yelverton covered 10.5 miles, ending at Princetown 1373 feet above sea level.

Yelverton Station, remains
Yelverton, November 2000. (John Earle)

The eventual closure of the line to Princetown in March 1956 did not pass without considerable local opposition and regret. Although the junction station at Yelverton survived for some years after this, the line to Princetown itself was disconnected in 1957.

Demolition of Yelverton Station began in 1964 after the track had been lifted – the latter operation featuring in many photographs by Sydney Taylor Jnr. A nature reserve has been established on the station site today, which is now private property with no public admittance. Seen through the foliage in this picture is the original accommodation bridge from which one local girl recalls waving to engine drivers as they passed beneath – and spitting on them from above if they didn't wave back!

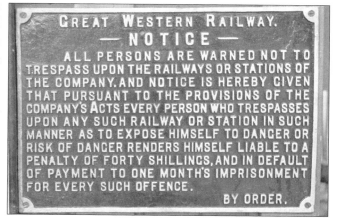

Great Western Railway notice at Yelverton Station, 1934.

(Tay3449)

Yelverton Station and Tunnel
Yelverton, 1934. Tay3474

A train of two autocars stands at the down platform of Yelverton Station in 1934. In the distance is the cutting and tunnel mouth on the line to Horrabridge. The tunnel runs for 641 yards underneath the village of Yelverton, an engineering feat of no little note, and one of which that most of those who drive through Yelverton today are entirely oblivious. At the northern end of the tunnel trains emerged into a deep cutting. The tunnel is dead straight and from one end a spot of daylight can be glimpsed at the other.

Horrabridge Station in 1914.

(Tay1486)

Yelverton Station and Tunnel
Yelverton, November 2000. (John Earle)

The tunnel remains intact but evidence of the station platforms and buildings is difficult to define. In less than fifty years since the station was closed nature has pretty much reclaimed her own. The edges of original platforms are still discernable – these were once paved with granite flagstone, later covered with tarmacadam. Thanks to photographs such as these it is possible to recreate a vision of the great railway enterprises on Dartmoor, now gone forever.

The Devil's Elbow
Princetown, 1929. Tay292

This is the main east-west road across the moor from Moretonhampstead to Yelverton, south-west of Princetown. Earliest photographs show roads in this area to be rough trackways, rutted and dusty in summer, quagmires in winter. It was at the spot known as Devil's Bridge, visible in the midground of this photograph, that the bodies of three soldiers were found who had been caught in a blizzard in 1853. They had walked from Dousland to Princetown in deep snow, stumbling to their deaths just a few hundred yards from the Duchy Hotel.

The road into Princetown from the south, taken on 1 June 1889 by Robert Burnard. The state of the track indicates the difficulties of moorland travel.

(Robert Burnard)

Note how well-defined is the field wall to the left of the road as it climbs the distant hill. The feature on the horizon is a bridge spanning the railway line as it enters Princetown at Peek Hill.

The Devil's Elbow
Princetown the B3212, February 2001. (Bryan Harper)

Negotiating this notorious bend was once an 'event' for those crossing the moor by car. Eventually its dangers proved too much for the authorities who ordered that it be eliminated. This took place in 1964 when the bridge at Peek Hill was demolished and, according to Kath Brewer in her book *The Railways, Quarries and Cottages of Fogginter* (Orchard Publications nd), '1150 tons of debris were transported to fill in Devil's Elbow'.

Comparison of the two photographs shows how much the road has been elevated in order to iron-out the sharpness of the original bend. This fills in the valley floor where the turned-up ground reveals considerable evidence of earlier mining activity.

The field wall is less distinct these days, while a plantation on the horizon acts as a shelter from prevailing south-westerlies for houses on the outer edge of Princetown.

The ribbon of tarmac along the road surface is evidence of trunking work, the laying of optic cables that has taken place nation-wide since the early 1990s. Thus, while travel is limited to 40mph above ground, below it moves at the speed of light!

Ockery Clapper Bridge
Near Princetown, 1936. Tay366

The B3212, a little way after leaving Princetown towards Two Bridges is carried over the Blacka Brook by a turnpike bridge known as Trena Bridge. Beside this, on the downstream side, stands the massive clapper known as Ockery (Oakery) Bridge. This served as a crossing point on the pack horse route that emerged south-westward from the Chagford–Tavistock track at Two Bridges.

Here, on the right bank, Thomas Tyrwhitt built a two-storey cottage c.1805 for use by French officers on parole from the prison at Princetown. In her book *Dartmoor Forest Farms*, Elisabeth Stanbrook provides a detailed account of the Ockery and of its later occupants, among them the Kistle family, who lived there from the 1840s to 1914. Their story is brought up to date in the Aune Head Arts newsletter of January 2001, in a letter received from Joan Taber of Denver, Colorado.

> *The earlier generation at Oakery Cottage were my grandparents, Eliza and James Kistle, stone mason and farmer. They married in 1841 and Oakery Cottage became their home. The Dartmoor Poet Jonas Coker [sic] was witness at their wedding in Lydford and he built some of the newtake walls at Oakery.*

Ockery Clapper Bridge
Near Princetown, November 2000. (Bryan Harper)

The bridge shows little sign of change, although the rudimentary parapet has disappeared in relatively recent times. Certainly it was there up to the late 1960s when the watercolourist S.R. Badmin captured the bridge in paint. The shaping of the stones on the central pier act as a cutwater, preserving the bridge from the full force of the river in flood.

Hoo Meavy, miner's cottage
Meavy Parish, 1935. Tay35131

Just as this cottage caught the eye of Sydney Taylor Jnr in 1935, so it earlier attracted Robert Burnard who took the photograph on the right in February 1889. Thus the Taylor photograph spans the hundred years or so between the oldest image and that shown below, with a number of details of interest to be seen in each image.

A further photograph reproduced in Pauline Hemery's *The Book Meavy,* and thought to have been taken c.1900, reveals a new slate roof, suggesting the time at which thatch was abandoned. The book records that when the Hoo Meavy estate was sold in 1833 it included the sale of Wheal Fanny Mine, described as producing 'tin of quality for richness not exceeded in any mine in the West of England.' Perhaps this explains the relative refinement of the cottage.

Robert Burnard's photograph, taken in 1889, shows the building was thatched at that time.

(Robert Burnard)

Hoo Meavy, miner's cottage
Meavy Parish, November 2000. (John Earle)

The cottage is built of granite and metamorphic stone (slate). The little building at the end is possibly a wash house which held the copper used for heating water. In the Burnard photograph smoke is coming from the chimney (washing hangs on the line). As the photograph opposite shows, the chimney has since been taken down.

The door where the little building meets the main cottage has been replaced with a hanging door but otherwise the original structure, even down to the singular guttering arrangement, is quite recognisable. Note how the configuration of the windows differs from the Burnard photograph.

Today the cottage bears a plaque claiming fifteenth-century mining origins, against which the Victorian lampstandard is a period piece out of its time.

Marchant's or Meavy Bridge
Meavy Parish, 1940. Tay4016a

The original crossing point on the River Meavy, just below the village, was the ford and stepping stones; those following the road to the bridge are obliged to execute a sharp loop. When Anna Eliza Bray and her husband visited Meavy in 1831 she wrote:

> *...we walked down to the bridge: It is formed of one high arch that crosses a beautiful river, where we watched the trout playing about for some time since such was the perfect purity and cleanness of the stream, we could see them as plainly as if they were gold and silver fish in a glass globe of water.*

The graceful arch is typical of the bridges crossing Dartmoor rivers on the lower moorland slopes. Often on old packhorse routes, these single-arch bridges are built with winter rains in mind, providing a span that allows the boiling flood to flow beneath without damage to the bridge abutments and foundations.

Marchant's or Meavy Bridge
Meavy Parish, December 2000. (John Earle)

Such bridges have attracted the eye of artists and photographers on the moor through the ages and the Taylors were no exception. Among the photographs in their collection are many of this type – the presence of the bridge adding a pleasing focal point to an enduring country scene.

However, Meavy Bridge, like many of its type, was not constructed to withstand the demands of modern traffic. Increasingly such bridges are subject to accidental damage and wear, particularly from lorries and farm vehicles. Though superficial, perhaps just the dislodgement of stones from a parapet, unsympathetic repairs can spoil the aesthetic lines of the original.

Meavy Bridge shows some signs of such repair. In common with many other bridges of this type, the structure is reinforced for the demands of modern traffic with tie rods through its width.

Sticklepath
Sticklepath Parish, 1934. Tay344

Before the much-disputed construction of the dual carriageway which now skirts the moor's northern edge, the main A30 route wound its tortuous way through the little villages of Whiddon Down, South Zeal and Sticklepath before descending into Okehampton, a notorious bottleneck for summer traffic from the 1950s to the 1970s. Taking this same route today it is astounding that these inadequate roads and narrow village streets were subjected to such a continuous barrage of noise and pollution.

This photograph was taken in pre-war days, when the cost of cars, such as the little Austin seen on the right, was only just within reach of ordinary families. The road has no markings and the presence of the blossoming flowerbeds in front of the cottages, each with its door opening directly on to the street, speak of sleepy village life, untrammelled by heavy traffic.

Thatched roofs show an interesting variety of patchwork repairs.

Sticklepath
Sticklepath Parish, November 2000. (Bryan Harper)

Pavements protect pedestrians from the traffic while white lines and roadsigns are awkward concessions to the rule of the motor car. But remove the parked cars from the scene and significant changes are hearteningly few. Street furniture (the ugly lamp posts here), as planners call it, proliferates in all our villages – improving amenities perhaps, but often to the detriment of the view.

TV aerials sprout from every rooftop (soon to be replaced by satellite dishes?) but these are temporary in the overall scheme of things. The bench outside the Devonshire Inn implies a pleasant drink outside is possible – unlikely a couple of decades ago. If evidence were put forward to support the building of bypasses this might be it.

The Devonshire Inn as it looked c.1909. One of the many photographs in South Tawton and South Zeal with Sticklepath *by Roy and Ursula Radford (published by Halsgrove, 2000).*

The West Okement River, Okehampton
Okehampton, 1934. Tay3416b

Availability of water is one of the factors governing settlement and, although moorland streams are plentiful, much ingenuity has been expended on Dartmoor over the centuries to ensure a convenient and constant supply to town and farm. But the course of a river through a town posed problems in terms of containment in times of flood, and in matters of health where local industries and the general population used watercourses as convenient means of waste disposal.

Industrial processes associated with mining, tanning and the woollen industry were often reliant upon an ample supply of water; their by-products were sometimes dangerously pollutant. In past times a blind eye was turned to these problems until the community was faced by the stench from polluted streams in summer, or an outbreak of cholera. With the Industrial Revolution giving rise to more chemical processing such problems increased throughout the nineteenth century and continued well into the twentieth.

Here, with its moorland background, the West Okement meanders at the bottom of the deep channel over which buildings project on either side. Note the fuel tank on the left – a pollution incident waiting to happen.

The West Okement River, Okehampton
Okehampton, November 2000. (Bryan Harper)

Today we are more conscious of environmental issues and one of the major achievements of the past few decades has been the laws passed to control pollution from industrial waste. The Environment Agency and associated bodies are on hand to act quickly on isolated pollution incidents and to apply the law where necessary. However, fines in the case of incidents of river pollution do little to restore the damage done to wildlife and the environment in general. Despite the law, rivers and streams are commonly used as dumping grounds, the last resting place of many a supermarket trolley.

Here in full spate the river has a more natural look to it. Gone are the industrial premises, replaced by housing, while the riverbank on the right, where it has been reinforced, is attractively landscaped.

Owley Corner and Scad Brook
South Brent, 1941. Tay4124

The Ordnance Survey maps of Dartmoor show a network of newtake walls spreading out to meet the open moor. Where the angle of a wall protrudes on to the commons the name 'Corner' is sometimes applied, as at Batworthy Corner, and Glasscombe Corner. Eric Hemery (*High Dartmoor*) waxes lyrical about Owley Corner and this little visited area of the moor:

> *No more beautiful valley lies on the fringe of high Dartmoor than this... By far the most attractive approach from the border country is Owley Lane, where the all-sheltering walls are kept in repair, rather than left to crumble and be replaced by wire, by the brothers French of Owley and Coryndon Farms. The colourful scene from Owley Gate on a spring day ranges through the dark purple of Three Burrows, the mottled slope of Wacka Tor, the emerald green of the enclosures on the Glaze peninsula, the fields of Coryndon dotted with the grey and white of ewes and new born lambs, and the many shades of green...*

Owley Corner and Scad Brook
South Brent, January 2001. (John Earle)

Some of Hemery's springtime delights are missing from this wintery view. Patches of snow lie in the valley folds, remnant of the falls that brought a white Christmas to Dartmoor for the first time for many years. The little stream and ford are hidden by gorse, but the pattern of the landscape is unchanged. However, with pressure on farms one wonders how much longer the traditional stone walls will be maintained as Hemery relates, out of a sense of tradition. Although grants are given for such work, it could never be that all the miles of moorland wall could thus be preserved, and the obvious reason for Owley Corner's name may, in the distant future, be obscured.

Duckspool Letterbox and Crossing's Memorial
OS 625679, 1952. Tay5215a

Duckspool, as the name implies, was thought to have been a haunt of wildfowl on the moor, until tinners are said to have drained the shallow pool. It is in many respects the southern moor's equivalent of Cranmere Pool to the north, not least in the presence of a famous letterbox. That at Duckspool was set up in 1938 by an avid group of walkers (H.T. Franks, Dr Malim, and a party known as Dobson's Moormen). They fixed to the large boulder here a bronze plaque as a memorial to the author William Crossing. In 1963 came a second memorial commemorating the life of Charles Carpenter, a founder member of Dobson's Moormen.

The contents of Duckspool letter-box when photographed by Sydney Taylor in 1952.

(Tay 5215b)

This photograph was taken in 1952, fourteen years after the letterbox was set up but it is probable that visits to the area were infrequent. Sydney Taylor and his colleagues found the contents of the box worthy of a separate photograph, and no doubt duly signed the book before leaving.

Duckspool Letterbox and Crossing's Memorial
OS 625679, January 2001. (John Earle)

Today letterboxing provides a healthy and enjoyable way of exploring the moor for many keen 'letterboxers'. An association exists and a number of successful books relating to the search for letterboxes have been published. All this started from the famous Cranmere postbox set up in 1854 by James Perrott – a glass jar in which those intrepid enough to reach Cranmere could signal their achievement by leaving a visiting card. Modern letterboxes take the form of stout metal cases (often army surplus ammunition boxes) which contain a book and a rubber stamp – the latter for marking in one's own book evidence of having found the site.

The bronze plaque set up on the boulder at Duckspool in memory of William Crossing. Photographed in 1952.

(Tay 5215c)

There is a down side to letterboxers. Not all those who take part do so with due consideration for others, while certain popular sites in summer resemble a beehive such is the to-ing and fro-ing. Serious walkers tend to look down on letterboxers – without any good cause.

The photograph shows some dramatic erosion around 'Crossing's' boulder, perhaps a sign of the number of visitors who now reach these remote parts of the moor with increasing regularity.

Huckworthy Bridge
Sampford Spiney, c.1910. TayWB24

This ancient and graceful structure is given only brief notice in Pevsner's *Devon*: 'very narrow with cutwaters'. It is a typical packhorse bridge, complete with niches to allow pedestrians an escape should they meet with a train of packhorses crossing the bridge.

Here, the bridge hung with ivy, there is little wonder that this scene captured the eye of the photographer, so idyllic is it. Robert Burnard found the view captivating too, while his photograph, taken in May 1891, shows more of the houses on the far bank. Note that in his photograph there are fields behind the houses, obscured by woodland today. Note too how closely the trees have encroached upon the bridge itself in the present day photograph.

Huckworthy Bridge
Sampford Spiney, November 2000, (Bryan Harper)

The present-day view is just as captivating, so much so that a seat has been provided for the enjoyment of passers-by.

Robert Burnard took his photograph of Huckworthy on 30 May 1891.

(Robert Burnard)

The Oxenham Arms
South Zeal, 1926. Tay261

The original building is thought to date from the twelfth century but it was not licensed as a public house until the late fifteenth century. Later, after rebuilding, it was the property of the Burgoyne family and then came into the hands of the Oxenhams, after whom the inn gets its name. This family is associated with the legend of the white bird, made famous by Charles Kingsley in *Westward Ho!* The appearance of the bird was said to herald a death in the Oxenham family and tragically this came about on the eve of the wedding of Lady Margaret Oxenham when the bird appeared, not to her, but to her father. Next day, at the altar, the Lady was killed by a jealous lover. In their recent book on South Zeal, Roy and Ursula Radford provide a little more factual evidence of the inn's past, relating that in the eighteenth and nineteenth centuries it served passengers travelling on the mail coaches that rumbled into the village on their arduous journeys east or west.

The inn is said to be built over a prehistoric menhir of giant proportions, part of which is visible in one of the bar-room walls. Though people have tried digging downwards, the full size of the enormous stone has never been determined!

The Oxenham Arms
South Zeal, November 2000. (Bryan Harper)

Apart from superficial changes the inn has retained all or most of its late sixteenth-century appearance, although the porch is a later addition. The stone mullioned windows and the huge lintel over the carriageway entrance on the left give this building a solid and handsome facade.

The roof exhibits the greatest change since 1926 when it was beginning to show signs of age. Gone too is the obtrusive telephone pole.

Note the inn sign in the earlier picture extending as far out towards the road as possible as if to demand that patrons stop. There was certainly fierce competition from a number of other public houses in the village at one time.

Fice's (Fitz) Well
Okehampton Hamlets, 1934. Tay3415a

Situated a short distance south-east of Okehampton, the cross lies in that part of the moor known as Okehampton Park.

The origins of the cross are shrouded in legend and it is often confused with Fitz's Well near the Blacka Brook at Princetown. One authority has it that the cross came originally from St Michael's Chapel at Halstock a few hundred yards east of its present location – the chapel already being described as ruinous during the sixteenth century.

One legend concerns a husband and wife lost upon the moor, convinced that they were under a spell that could only be broken by drinking water. They stumbled on a small pool on the site of the present well which saved the day – and erected the cross in thanksgiving.

A similar story is attached to the name of Sir John Fitz who is connected to both this and the Princetown well by name.

At one time the Okehampton well was known as Spicer's Well.

Fice's (Fitz) Well
Okehampton Hamlets, January 2001. (John Earle)

Much trampling around the site of the cross, whether by people or livestock, has given the area a barren look. But the little cross (less than a metre in height) seems sturdy enough.

William Crossing tells a story of young people visiting the well on Easter morning in order that they might partake of the waters which gave them the power to see their destiny.

At one time the cross lay fallen at this spot but was re-erected around 1900.

The view from here is spectacular.

Foggintor Quarry

near Princetown, 1942. Taymisc48.4247

The construction of the Plymouth & Dartmoor Railway in the 1820s opened up Dartmoor to those who wished to exploit its mineral resources. There was great demand for granite, both for the construction of the dockyard at Devonport and for the Plymouth Breakwater for which 3.5 million tons of stone were required. The railway stimulated the opening of a number of quarries on the western side of the moor: Ingra Tor, Great and Little Kings Tor, Swell Tor, Crip Tor and Foggintor.

Kath Brewer provides a fascinating history of the quarry in her book *The Railways, Quarries and Cottages of Foggintor.* Having lived at the quarry as a child before the demolition of the cottages there – some of which are seen in Sydney Taylor's photograph – she is able to provide a first hand account. The last of the dwellings were demolished in the early 1950s and only their ruins now remain.

Foggintor Quarry

near Princetown, January 2001. (John Earle)

A bleak prospect but a truly memorable place to have spent one's childhood amid the freedom of the moor. For well over a century stone quarrying provided work for hundreds and created an industrial land-scape within the heart of the moor. The scene forms an important part of what is now the moor's indus-trial heritage and calls will surely one day be made to protect what remains, just as earlier calls were made to tear down the 'grave disfigurement' of the quarry buildings.

Ruined buildings at Foggintor today.

(John Earle)

The television mast, a modern disfigurement, stands on North Hessary Tor.

Black Tor Falls Blowing House
Walkhampton Parish, 1934. Tay34126

The blowing house was an on-site industrial unit used for producing smelted tin from ore. They were first used around the fourteenth century. They were a sophisticated processing plant, albeit using crude materials found on site: stone and turf for the building, water to power a small wheel which in turn fanned bellows to heat the tinners' furnace. Layers of crushed ore and charcoal were laid inside the furnace and, when at melting point, the tin would flow into a hollow stone from where it would be transferred into moulds.

This process, developed over a considerable period, produced tin of an exceptional purity.

The ore was crushed on a mortar stone using a variety of methods, some mechanical, which resulted in rounded hollows being created in the stone. When these were too deep to allow efficient crushing, the stone was turned over and the new face worked. Discarded mortar stones are often found alongside blowing houses, including this house at Black Tor Falls.

Black Tor Falls Blowing House
Walkhampton Parish, January 2001. (John Earle)

There are two tinners' buildings at this location, one on each side of the river. One had the Roman numerals XIII carved in a lintel above the door – the significance of which is not known.

There are some discarded mortar stones lying about, but as Stephen Woods records in his book *Dartmoor Stone* (Devon Books, 1999), they have been moved around so much that it is difficult to say to which building they belonged. In view of this remark it is extraordinary how little these buildings have changed considering the numbers of people who now pass by.

However, a closer look at these two photographs reveals a number of stones missing from the upper walls.

Horrabridge Post Office
Horrabridge, 1934. Tay3477

The yard in the foreground is full of the artefacts and junk that are soon to be confined to history. The old farm wagons, craftsman made, and still very much in use in pre-war times, were to become quickly obsolescent as tractor power came in. Everywhere there are touches which speak plainly of the 1930s – elsewhere described as Devon's 'forgotten decade'. Adverts on the door to the right give notice of a display by the 'Air Dare Devil's', while the *Daily Express* gives an exclusive on Greta Garbo. Just visible on the distant shop front is an advertisement for Robin Starch.

A faded sign declares the Post Office once did teas.

Sydney Taylor Jnr took a great number of photographs of Horrabridge in the period before the Great War up to the 1960s, years in which the village was clearly undergoing major change, with many dwellings being demolished.

A photograph of a barn near Horrabridge, taken in 1914, contains some interesting details of agricultural life at that time.

(Tay 1426)

Horrabridge Post Office
Horrabridge, December 2000. (Bryan Harper)

The yard has become lawn and cars have replaced the wagons but most of the significant elements of the scene remain unchanged. The entranceway on the right now extends to the roofline but, apart from new roofing, the dwellings are instantly recognisable.

The post office endures, despite the demise of others in villages across the moor which has robbed people (particularly the elderly and infirm) of a meeting place at which cares and events can be brought to the notice of the community. Central government has awoken to the problems faced by communities who, without adequate public transport, are also bereft of their post office and stores – but in many cases their efforts come too late.

A signal on the railway line at Horrabridge, with a distant view towards Tavistock, 1912. The girder on the right is part of the old bowstring bridge which crossed the A386.

(Tay 1224)

Horrabridge, Jordan Lane

Horrabridge, 1967. Tay6716d

The closure of the railway line in 1962, not achieved without considerable opposition, brought fundamental changes to the lives of those who lived alongside. The ending of employment for railway staff and those associated with the line, the cessation of a means of transport to major work centres such as Plymouth and Tavistock, and the general sense of unease at losing what had once seemed so permanent, greatly affected people in villages such as Horrabridge.

Within a few years came the dismantling of the track and the demolition of bridges, signals, and the station itself. This too changed the face of Horrabridge, while road schemes and new housing added to the transformation.

Sydney Taylor's photographs are a vital record of this period of change.

Roadside cottages at Horrabridge, scheduled for demolition in 1967.

(Tay 6716a)

Horrabridge, Jordan Lane

Horrabridge, January 2001. (John Earle)

The Sampford Spiney road leading off to the right has been widened to accommodate modern traffic. The old building in the centre of Taylor's photograph has disappeared completely, with the house behind it being recognisable in the recent picture by the gable and chimneys.

The old finger post has gone to be replaced by no less than seven road and hydrant signs. An ugly (if more efficient) street light dangles over the road, while the electricity pole, festooned with cables, does little for the view.

Cottages in Horrabridge, overlooked by Wright's Stores, are due for demolition, 1967.

(Tay 6716b)

Almshouses, Moretonhampstead
Moretonhampstead, 1943. Tay4335

Unlike Horrabridge, featured in previous pages, some other Dartmoor towns and villages escaped major change throughout the twentieth century. Moretonhampstead is one of these. Though it too had to face the closure of its railway station, in 1959, the central core of the town has remained largely intact, and what might at one time have relegated this community to the status of rural backwater has in reality created for it an opportunity for carefully considered development through which its historic character can be preserved.

The almshouses are sited on the old Exeter road. They date from 1637 and are built in Jacobean style with an open gallery fronted by five arches on either side of the gallery entrance. At one time two of these archways were blocked up at either end of the building. Originally serving as the work-house, they later became the poorhouse and by the late 1930s had fallen into decay and were condemned. Thanks to a local benefactor, Mervyn Davie, the buildings were purchased by the town and renovated. Taylor's photograph was taken three years after this work was completed.

Almshouses, Moretonhampstead
Moretonhampstead, December 2000. (John Earle)

These two scenes show almost no change – and perhaps this is Moretonhampstead's greatest asset.

At the time this is written there are various plans afoot concerning the future development of Moretonhampstead. An active local group has made great strides towards making the centre of town more attractive, both to residents and visitors, but this is against the background of proposals to build 150 houses on the edge of the town.

There are any number of problems for planners to consider, not least how best to remove the pressure of traffic emerging from at least three major routes into a congested crossroad in the middle of the town. Solve this problem without too much disruption to the existing buildings, or by swamping the town with new housing, and Moretonhampstead will emerge as one of the eastern moor's most attractive places to live.

Eylesbarrow Mine
OS599681, 1937. Tay3730

Sydney Taylor captured, in 1937, the stark remains of what once was a major industrial site in the heart of the moor. A. K. Hamilton Jenkin in *Mines of Devon* (David & Charles, 1974) says of the mine:

Eylesborough or Eylesbarrow (pronounced Ailsboro), some two miles north-east of Sheepstor, was a tin mine of some importance, but records of its output are lacking and there are no known plans of the underground workings. The mine was at work in 1823 when, along with Vitifer and Whiteworks, it ranked among the few mines then active on Dartmoor. It had the further distinction of owning a smelting house where 100 blocks of tin metal were coined in the Michaelmas quarter of 1824. Under the name of Dartmoor Consolidated, exploratory work was in progress from 1838 until 1844 when due to the low price of black tin (£40 per ton) and the difficulty of renewing the lease, operations were suspended.

The mine was reopened in 1847, closed again a year later, only for workings to be restarted in 1849 and closed for good shortly after.

Used for crushing ore, this set of stamps at Kit mine, Sheepstor, was photographed in 1933.

(Tay 339)

Eylesbarrow Mine
OS599681, January 2001. (John Earle)

In 1847 the mine was reported to have a large 'mansion house', smelting house, a smithy and other buildings. The mansion ruins, actually the mine captain's house which later became a farmhouse, are still a prominent feature in this otherwise barren landscape. Other evidence of the mine survives in the form of a row of paired stones which carried a flat-rod system, driven by a 50-foot waterwheel, used to drain the mine.

Among the Taylor Collection are many photographs showing relics of mining on Dartmoor. These include general views such as this, along with details of structures and artefacts associated with individual mines. As part of the industrial archaeological record of the moor they are of great value.

One of the pairs of granite posts which carried the flat-rod system at Eylesbarrow Mine.

(John Earle)

Soussons Cairn Circle

Soussons Down, near Postbridge, 1936. Taymisc72.369

In his acclaimed series books *Dartmoor Atlas of Antiquities* (Devon Books, Volumes 1-5 1991-97) Jeremy Butler provides the most comprehensive published account of archaeology on the moor. The cairn circle at Soussons is detailed in the second volume, as follows:

> *On the edge of the plantation, almost a kilometre south of the Red Barrows, is one of the best known cairn circles on Dartmoor where for once the Forestry Commission has left a generous clearing around it. A circle of 22 earthfast stones with a diameter of 8.6 m surrounds the remains of a cist, of which the two side slabs alone remain visible. An interesting find was made here when the cist was excavated in 1903. A false floor of paving slabs had been laid below the earth infilling, concealing two large coils of human hair. This was taken as a comparatively recent manifestation of witchcraft, belief in which was still prevalent on Dartmoor in the early nineteenth century according to Mrs Bray. She quotes from her husband's journal for 1827 where he records that one of his tenants had recently destroyed a cist, apparently on White Tor, which also contained human hair 'clotted together amongst the earth and stones'.*

Soussons Cairn Circle

Soussons Down, near Postbridge, December 2000. (John Earle)

Cairns are prehistoric monuments often associated with stone rows on Dartmoor, and the 'cist' referred to above is a burial chamber comprising slabs of stone forming a granite box.

These photographs illustrate clearly the effect that planting conifer forests has had on the open moor, and the potential for damage to existing archaeological features. As Jeremy Butler points out, in the case of this circle, some effort has been made not to disturb the immediate site. Indeed the forest here makes a dramatic backdrop to the ancient stone circle, but no more so than in its solitary position on open moor seen in the earlier photograph.

Fernworthy Stone Circle
Fernworthy, near Postbridge, 1934. Tay34122

There is no doubt that when Sydney Taylor took this photograph in 1934 he was aware of the impending peril to the archaeology of the area from the infant forest that appears in the background. In the fifth and final volume of *Dartmoor Atlas of Antiquities* (Devon Books, 1997), Jeremy Butler confirms Taylor's worst fears:

> *After coming under Forestry Commission control in 1930 the planted area vastly increased to include the important ceremonial complex on Froggymead Hill centred on a stone circle, one of the best surviving double alignments at Assycombe, the south western portion of Shoveldown field system, as well as a number of other settlements, cairns, enclosures, and field systems, all without any comprehensive survey beforehand. Some sites have been lost for good like the settlements said to occupy the slopes above Fernworthy stone circle, while others over-planted have now re-emerged in much poorer shape, like the Hemstone Rocks hut group originally probably part of the Shoveldown field system but now totally isolated within the trees. Even those few sites allotted a tiny clearing as a token concession to conservation have deteriorated considerably in the degraded environment surrounding them.*

Fernworthy Stone Circle
Fernworthy, December 2000. (John Earle)

It would be impossible to replicate Taylor's photograph, so much has the landscape in this area changed. However, this picture taken inside the forest gives some indication of the effect such planting might have upon existing archaeological features.

While the mechanical scarifying of the soil prior to planting in itself causes considerable damage, the growth of trees pushes aside stones and walls, disrupting their original structure. Harvesting of timber and replanting compounds the damage.

View over Powdermills

near Postbridge, 1969. Tay692e

The photographer stands with his back to the conifer forests that clad the slopes of Lakehead Hill and surround Bellever Tor. The trans-moorland B3212 here dips down towards Higher Cherry Brook Bridge on its way to Two Bridges. In the distance is Longaford Tor.

Central to the view is the settlement of Powdermills, the cluster of buildings seen in the middle distance. It was here in 1844 that Plymouthian George Frean started to manufacture gunpowder on a large scale for use in mines, and for military use.

The remote location of the site made it ideal as far as the possibility of accidental explosions was concerned, while an ample supply of water, brought here by leat, was essential to the processing of the raw materials. The local availability of peat, used in drying the gunpowder, was also a factor in choosing the site.

One of two chimney stacks at Powdermills, photographed in 1969. The height of these stacks ensured that sparks were taken well away from any of the buildings vulnerable to fire.

(Tay692a)

View over Powdermills

near Postbridge, December 2000. (Bryan Harper)

Powdermills is owned by the Duchy of Cornwall and was leased from the estate throughout its time as a gunpowder mill. The invention of dynamite brought an end to gunpowder and the mills closed in the late 1890s.

Today some of the buildings house a pottery which attracts tourists en route across the moor. Local Devon clays are used in the making of a variety of art and domestic pottery, fired in a kiln at the rear of the buildings, with the work of a number of potters on display.

In recent times repairs have been done to save the fabric of the old mill buildings from further deterioration, although their massive size had kept them generally sound. Indeed, apart from their missing roofs (which anyway were deliberately flimsy in order to direct explosions upwards), they remain remarkably intact.

Conifers still line the left hand side of the road, sweeping back over the moor. The stone walls on the Powdermills side of the road have recently undergone some major renovation work, but the scene overall is unchanged.

Proof Mortar, Powdermills
near Postbridge, 1969. Tay692b

The cast iron proof mortar at Powdermills, when photographed by Sydney Taylor in 1969, still retained its original fittings, although its wooden frame had long since rotted away leaving it lying rather forlornly on its granite bed.

The mortar was used to test the gunpowder manufactured here with a (probably) granite ball of a known weight being fired using various charges of powder in order to ascertain its explosive strength.

As an artefact connected with an important part of Dartmoor's history the mortar was recognised by the National Park Authority as being worthy of repair and in the 1980s they commissioned its renovation under the supervision of Austin C. Carpenter, world authority on the restoration and conservation of historic guns, who happened to live locally.

Proof Mortar, Powdermills
near Postbridge, December 2000. (Bryan Harper)

In his book *Cannon* (Halsgrove, 1993), Austin Carpenter describes the work done on the mortar in order to bring it to its present condition. In the course of this work the letter Z was discovered faintly cast into the trunnion, indicating its origin. Although the weapon resembled a type made at Woolwich in the mid 1800s, the letter Z was known to have been the maker's mark of George Matthews of Shropshire and it is possibly from his foundry that the piece was commissioned.

The mortar today stands at the side of the track leading in to Powdermills. The wooden bed on which it stands is a replica of a pattern known to have been used for this type of mortar. It is set up at an elevation of 45°, as was standard for such pieces.

On completion of its restoration Carpenter procured a stone shot which was fired twice from the mortar, 'with impressive results'!

Two photographs of buildings at Powdermills, taken in 1969. They show the massive construction of the walls, built to withstand accidental explosions, while roof structures were deliberately light in construction thus directing any blast upwards and out of harm's way. The centre section of the building housed a waterwheel powered from water carried in a leat, remains of which can be seen in the lower photograph.

(Tay692c and 692d)

Redford Farm
Willsworthy, 1920. Tay2018

Though one of the few poor quality photographs in the Taylor Collection, this is also one of the more important. It shows the remains of Redford Farm which lay in the shadow of White Tor at Willsworthy.

Eden Phillpotts uses the setting in his novel *The Whirlwind*, in which he calls the farm Ruddyford, a name close to that given locally – Reddaford or Ruddiver. It is known that in the early 1800s the farm was occupied by a John Kennard, and the whole area is rich in the remains of earlier settlements and mining activity.

The scene is barely recognisable as a Dartmoor settlement, with its unusually high wall surrounding the farm having more the appearance of an African kraal. The establishment of the Willsworthy Range, around 1900, signalled the end of the farm, which has thus not only suffered the misfortunes of natural decay but has been subjected to a more systematic dilapidation at the hands of the military. Ten years before this photograph the house was described as being in ruins while the paraphernalia of a firing range, including a target railway and observation post, much disturbed the land around.

Redford Farm
Willsworthy, January 2001. (John Earle)

In *High Dartmoor*, Eric Hemery describes the layout of the original site:

> *The farmhouse occupied a level site on a shelf above the left bank of the brook, and signs are that its medieval forerunner measured thirty feet by fifteen. The gate at the farm entrance was customarily kept closed, and there was a sheep creep within a few yards of its site. Adjacent to the farmhouse is a rectangular platform, thirty feet by ten, and at its north end a circular depression in the ground, twenty-three feet in diameter and having a central hollow. This could have been a corn-grinding mill with the usual timber upright and revolving crusher: the platform was almost certainly a windstrew.*

The ruins at Redford Farm, 1931.

(Tay311)

Today turf-covered mounds barely define the outline of the original settlement.

Longstone (Langstone) Manor
Burrator, 1935. Tay35128

The Taylors' fascination with the area around Burrator sprang from a realisation of the need to capture the changes wrought to the landscape as a result of the construction of the reservoir. This was first opened in 1898, but in 1926 the dam was heightened, prior to which the leases on many of the farms in the catchment area were terminated.

Longstone Manor was one of the farms abandoned around this time, and was clearly a shell at the time this photograph was taken in 1935. The ruins and the garden wall with its archway reflect something of the manor's refinement, although in the late 1700s when it became a farm it was much altered from the original form.

Eric Hemery suggests the name is taken from a lost menhir now submerged by the reservoir.

The ruined wall at Longstone, photographed in 1914.

(Tay1464)

Longstone (Langstone) Manor
Burrator, December 2000. (John Earle)

The manor house today bears a notice warning of the dangerous state of the building as it enters its final stages of decay. Hemery writes that behind the house there stands a windstrew (on which grain was threshed), the ruins of a cider house, and several granite troughs. Some of the massive gateposts that once served the farm also stand around the house while, inside, huge fireplaces can still be seen.

These days carved granite of any type is prey to thieves, and such ruins are in danger of being robbed. This has always been so, with the fall of grand houses serving as a convenient source of stone for new building. However, it seems less acceptable when such things as mortar stones and pig troughs are removed from the context of their origins, ending up as high-priced garden ornaments in suburbia.

The windstrew at Longstone, photographed in 1914. This was the manor threshing floor. On one of the steps is carved 'J.E. 1640'.

(Tay1465)

Mary Tavy Station
Mary Tavy, 1914. Tay1446

Mary Tavy and Blackdown was the first station on the line north out of Tavistock en route to Launceston. The photograph shows the single track line and the platform buildings, including a signal box and waiting room. After the L&SWR opened its independent line to Plymouth, the signal box and crossing loop at Mary Tavy were taken out of use in 1892, but the down line remained as a 'poultry run'. In 1905 there was a complaint that the station master had neglected the appearance of the station and the following year new shrubs were planted. The station was finally put out of use in 1948 although the waiting room survived in a ruinous state until the late 1950s.

A woman waves from the garden of Station Cottage, Mary Tavy, 1914.

(Tay1447)

Mary Tavy Station Cottage
Mary Tavy, December 2000. (Bryan Harper)

The principal elements of the Station Cottage, as photographed by Sydney Taylor, can still be recognised in the present-day view, although a number of extensions have been added since 1914.

It is as though the track and the platform had never existed.

Lew Manor
Lewtrenchard, 1937. Tay371a

Devon, and particularly Dartmoor, is not blessed with grand houses. Even castles converted for domestic use and stately homes in Devon tend to be more compact than their counterparts in counties northward.

Even Lew Manor is not what it appears to be, and is what Pevsner describes as 'an intriguing confection' created by the Rev. Sabine Baring-Gould who lived here from 1881. From its humbler original Baring-Gould constructed the Jacobean-style manor we see today, without the aid of professional architect or builder, but employing local craftsmen whom he had trained.

Interestingly it has been suggested that a miniature granite cloister at the back of the building is based on the almshouses at Moretonhampstead (see page 108).

In many ways the house reflects Baring-Gould himself – an extraordinary eclectic who pursued interests ranging from archaeology to collecting folk songs. A friend and colleague of many of the late Victorian Dartmoor antiquarians and enquirers, he would almost certainly have been acquainted with one or more of the Taylor family. He died in 1924.

The impressive porch at Lew Manor, 1937.

(Tay371c)

Lew Manor
Lewtrenchard, December 2000. (Bryan Harper)

Today Lew Manor is an hotel with a considerable reputation; BMWs and Mercedes have replaced the Rileys and Morrises seen parked in the Taylor photograph.

It is amazing how little the fabric of the building or the surrounding gardens have altered over the years; a tribute in part to the skill of Baring-Gould and his workmen. In 1928 the famed Gertrude Jekyll advised on the layout of the gardens and they remain an attractive setting for this unusual house with its strong Dartmoor connections.

The lake in the foreground is sited on old quarry workings.

The Rev. Sabine Baring-Gould oversees archaeological work at Grimspound, 1899.

(Robert Burnard)

Tomb of John Godden

Sampford Spiney, 1915. Tay1520

John Godden's family tomb sits in Sampford Spiney churchyard like a cuckoo in a nest. In its sombre shadow stand the more modest gravestones of local folk but, other than the marble tablets affixed to its sides, there are no clues to explain the imposing incongruity of the Godden mausoleum. Dartmoor churchyard grave markers tend to be simple, often of moorstone, this tomb is clearly exceptional.

Several thousand years separate the subject of this photograph with another Taylor photograph of the cist at Lakehead Hill – the prestige burial chamber of *its* day.

The cist at Lakehead Hill, 1933.

(Tay 6729a)

Tomb of John Godden

Sampford Spiney, December 2000. (Bryan Harper)

The church of St Mary is a gem among moorland border churches, hidden in a quiet fold.

It is surprising to find a tomb as grand as this in a village churchyard on Dartmoor, and no doubt for this reason it caught the photographer's eye. In any event, examples of such design are rare in Devon, notable by their scarcity in fact.

The memorial to John Godden reads simply: 'in loving memory of John Godden, born 22 September 1849, died 14 February 1938.'

One of the marble plaques attached to Godden's tomb. It is a memorial to Anna Maria Godden, John's wife, who died tragically young.

(author)

Sheepstor Church Lychgate
Sheepstor Parish, 1934. Tay34183

The lychgate is traditionally the place at which a coffin is rested before entering the church sanctuary. The central stone and the double entrance here would allow pallbearers to pass through the gate and on into the churchyard.

In the graveyard here are the memorials to James Brooke, the first Rajah of Sarawak (d.1868) and his son, the second Rajah (d.1917). The first has a massive sarcophagus of red Aberdeen granite, while his son's memorial is a huge moorstone boulder for which part of the churchyard wall was removed so that it might be emplaced.

The church of St Leonard, Sheepstor, with the lychgate glimpsed beyond the cross.

Sheepstor Church Lychgate
Sheepstor Parish, November 2000. (John Earle)

Much of the timber on the lychgate has been renewed, the slate replaced on the roof and a piece of guttering added. The main lintel is the same, which says something for the durability of oak, for even in 1934 it looked a little worse for wear. Some paving has been laid in the entranceway.

On the day of his visit the photographer John Earle was told that the gate on the right had recently to be replaced as the old one was knocked down by a bullock that had wandered into the churchyard!

Runnage Bridge
near Postbridge, 1948. Tay483

Taylor refers to this as Pizwell Bridge but it is certainly the structure today known as Runnage Bridge. In fact it stands almost exactly halfway between these two ancient tenements; the OS map confirms it as Runnage Bridge.

It is the crossing point of the Walla Brook on the old road between Postbridge and Widecombe-in-the-Moor which winds over Soussons Down. The original clapper bridge is easily discerned under what Hemery describes as its 'hideous parapet', but one assumes general strengthening has taken place in order to cope with modern traffic.

The brook runs gently down to Pizwell Steps along a meadow-like stretch of riverbank ideal for picnics. However, a series of granite posts now prevent cars driving on to the grass – a necessary precaution against erosion.

A Taylor family picnic on Dartmoor, 1941. This must have been a particular treat as wartime petrol rationing curtailed a good deal of motoring for pleasure.

(Tay41102)

Runnage Bridge
near Postbridge, February 2001. (author)

The parapet of the bridge appears to have grown more solid, and no less ugly, since 1948, and the conifers in the background do nothing to improve the view. The whole scene has something of a suburban parkland feel about it – not an improvement. However, the prevention of cars parking here, as at similar sites elsewhere on the moor, can only be a good thing, not least for those resident nearby.

Pizwell, a photograph taken by Robert Burnard in 1889.

(Robert Burnard)

Gigley Bridge
Dean Prior, 1937. Tay3755

Another occasion on which the placename on the Ordnance Survey map differs to common use. The OS has it as Gidley Bridge, William Crossing and others as Gigley. Not that such variations should be standardised, for many a derivation has been lost through adoption of modern spellings. Much of this went on in the early days of mapmaking when surveyors interpreted names which hitherto had only been spoken, never written down.

Gigley bridge sits across the Harbourne River which rises in a spring at Dockwell on the southern edge of Dean Moor and winds its way across the South Hams to enter the Dart near Cornworthy. Not far from the bridge is the settlement of Skerraton, anciently *Sciredun,* which land was held on the provision of two arrows to the king whenever he hunted on Dartmoor.

Gigley Bridge
Dean Prior, November 2000. (Bryan Harper)

Another of the many single-span packhorse bridges on Dartmoor. In Sydney Taylor's photograph the summer sun lights the bridge in dappled shadow, the beech trees in full leaf. His wife and daughter pose for this delightful family picture.

The scene in winter is far less enticing, with the river swollen by recent rains. Note the ford to the left of the bridge – probably the original crossing point before the bridge was built, and still used by riders today.

Hemerdon Ball

near Plympton, 1934. Tay34151

Clumps, stands of trees on prominent hilltops, are not unusual in the border country of Dartmoor. Remnants of ancient woods, or deliberately planted as this clump appears to be, they remain as very particular landmarks in our countryside. Although standing outside the National Park boundary, Hemerdon Ball, at a height of 212m, is geologically very much Dartmoor. Nearby is Hemerdon Mine, a source of the tungsten mineral wolfram.

The view from Hemerdon Ball would provide a day's lessons for any teacher of life sciences: moors to the north, industrial clay wastes at Headon, the rich agricultural land to the south, and the urban sprawl of Plympton, recently said to be England's fastest expanding town, are all within compass.

Hanger Down Clump, a photograph by Sydney Taylor taken in 1928.

(Tay282)

Hemerdon Ball

near Plympton, December 2000. (John Earle)

Pressures from expanding towns such as Plympton on the edge of Dartmoor come from more than the simple spread of housing. People living close to the moor naturally use it as their 'back garden', thus adding to the numbers who visit. Noise and light pollution follow in the train of growing towns. In the early 1960s the population of Plympton was in the region of 12 000, today it numbers 40 000!

The view northwards over Plympton St Maurice towards Dartmoor, 1937. The white speck on the horizon is the clay tip at Headon.

(Tay3782b)

137

Shilston Farm
Throwleigh, 1947. Tay4711

Also called Higher Shilston, this is one of the more important vernacular buildings on Dartmoor and is discussed at some length by R. Hansford Worth in his book *Dartmoor* (David & Charles, 1967). A photograph and an illustration of the entrance appear in the book, along with a description of a number of the building's features. Hemery too extols the attractions of Shilston (Shilstone as he has it), the 'longhouse preserves intact many traditional features, including a fine trough and lipstone.'

The photograph is taken on the day of a visit by the Devonshire Association, of which Sydney was a keen member. It is possible that Worth was one of the party.

Shilston Farm
Throwleigh, January 2001. (John Earle)

Taylor's photograph appears to show the last days of a building in the left foreground, of which there is no sign in the recent view. Gone too are the trees that framed the house in 1947, but otherwise the building remains as it was – a superb example of a Dartmoor farmhouse.

A Devonshire Association outing to Shaugh Prior, 1934. R. Hansford Worth third from left.
(Tay3473)

Honeybag Tor from Chinkwell
Widecombe-in-the-Moor, 1946. Tay461

Such views as this are enduring and little has changed in the years between which these two photographs were taken. To the left of Honeybag Tor is Natsworthy Manor and the beautiful Heathercombe Valley. In his book *Heathercombe* (Westcountry Books, 1993), Claude Pikes provides a detailed study of this little known area of the moor which has been the site of human habitation for over four thousand years.

It was hereabouts that Crossing records a meeting between a landowner and a local inhabitant:

> *Chancing to meet an old woman he began talking about the place as though he were a stranger, and was told that one of the estates belong to Mr Blank, but that he did not live there continuously. Desirous of hearing what kind of reputation he had as a landlord, he asked her what sort of man Mr Blank was. "Can't tell 'e, sir,' replied the woman, 'Never seed 'n as I knaw by. But us call 'n ole darnin needle.'*

Honeybag Tor from Chinkwell
Widecombe-in-the-Moor, December 2000. (Bryan Harper)

In common with nearby Haytor, these tors are favoured by visitors who have to walk a relatively short distance to get here, and can keep the car in view! The ground around these tors, and the tracks up to them, bear the marks of many pairs of feet, and there are few days when figures cannot be spotted climbing on one height or another.

Blackslade Ford and Pil Tor
Widecombe-in-the-Moor, 1946. Tay463b

The monumental newtake walls on Blackslade Down funnel down to the Ford on Ruddycleave Water (Blackslade Water according to Hemery) at the foot of Blackslade Mire. This whole region is rich in sites of historical interest, among them Foales Arrishes, a network of prehistoric enclosures standing between the mire and Pil Tor (seen in the distance). Foale, it seems, was an innkeeper locally who used the fields here for keeping stock. An 'arrish' is a westcountry name for a stubble field.

Bear in mind the labour involved in building the walls seen here and some idea is given of the permanence and longevity of farming traditions on the moor.

Near the track are boundary stones inscribed with 'EPB 1837'. These describe the boundary between Blackslade and Buckland Manors, and the initials are those of Edmund Pollexfen Bastard, owner of the manor of Buckland.

Blackslade Ford and Pil Tor
Widecombe-in-the-Moor, December 2000. (John Earle)

Granite walls are of little practical use to modern farms and their upkeep costly in terms of man hours. Here the wall has been fenced with wire in order to keep stock from wandering. This is sheep country and certainly a Scotch Blackface would find the old walls no obstacle at all.

Eventually the stones will tumble back to earth and the walls disappear. Taylor's photographs will remain as an interesting record of how things once were.

Marjorie Taylor, Sydney's wife, at Blackslade, 1946.
(Tay363a)

Higher Mill, Peter Tavy
Peter Tavy, 1904. TayP723

This photograph is one of a number copied from postcards by Sydney Taylor. The original was taken by one of the Pearce family, postcard photographers of Plymouth, whom it is quite possible the Taylors knew. It shows the mill in 1904.

A mill has existed on this site from the fifteenth century, but the mill house was largely rebuilt in the early 1840s. Fortunately for this handsome building, the owners, whose family ties here are strong, appreciate its heritage. In the course of taking the contemporary photograph Mr Frank Collins provided Bryan Harper with some invaluable information relating to the history of Higher Mill and his family connection with it. This information will now be included with the Taylor Collection archive.

The little girl in the centre of the photograph is Elsie Edwards (mother of Frank Collins), and the girl on the right is Dolly Littlejohn who is holding Elsie's younger sister, Dorothy. In the mill door on the left is William Dodd, the Edwards children's uncle.

The mill ceased work in the early years of the twentieth century. It is now a listed building.

Higher Mill, Peter Tavy
Peter Tavy, February 2001. (Bryan Harper)

One of the purposes of this book is to encourage people to appreciate the value of photographs in terms of history. A photograph without a description of the event, place or people it portrays might be argued to be of less value in this sense. Fortunately, most of the photographs in the Taylor Collection are accompanied by a brief description, at least including the date and location.

In taking the contemporary photographs for use in this book and the accompanying exhibition both John Earle and Bryan Harper were met with openness and interest by those whose homes or villages they were photographing. This often led to additional information regarding the Taylor photograph, and sometimes provided an exact location of a place or building that had changed beyond recognition. In pursuing its aim of establishing a Dartmoor Archive, the Dartmoor Trust hopes to encourage and increase this bringing together of picture and story.

Drizzlecombe Menhir
Drizzlecombe, 1915. Tay158

One of the few photographs to portray the three principal members of the Taylor family photography dynasty, taken at Drizzlecombe in 1915. It shows Sydney Snr on the left, Frank, his brother, and Sydney Jnr on the right.

This book is dedicated to their work.

Drizzlecombe Menhir
Drizzlecombe, 14 February 2001. (Julian Davidson)

A lighthearted tribute to the 1915 photograph, with left to right, John Earle, Bryan Harper and Simon Butler.

It is interesting to compare what was considered to be necessary walking gear in 1915, and today.

The endpiece overleaf shows Frank Taylor at Swincombe, 1914.

Endpieces

A selection of photographs from the Taylor Collection not appropriate for comparison 'then and now' in the previous section, but which are of particular historical interest and show the wide range of Dartmoor subjects covered by the collection.

There are a number of photographs in the Taylor Collection the subjects of which are not identified, or perhaps misidentified where writing on the negative is difficult to decipher. The cottage on the left appears to be identified as 'Two Bridges, Widecombe', but no sign of the lane or cottage can be found in that area. The photograph is undated, believed to be c.1900.

(TayBB47a)

The farmhouse in the photograph below is also unidentified. It is hoped that by publishing such images information concerning them will come forward.

(TayBB46)

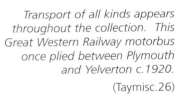

Transport of all kinds appears throughout the collection. This Great Western Railway motorbus once plied between Plymouth and Yelverton c.1920.

(Taymisc.26)

People figure in only a small number of photographs in the Taylor Collection, but this exception shows the signalman at Brentor Station, a Mr Blackmore, in 1913.

(Taymisc.100)

Sparkwell Mill, near Plympton, 1934. Taylor records that a casting on the wheel is inscribed 'Philip Veale, Millwright, Walkhampton.'

(Tay3497)

The clapper bridge at Fernworthy.

(TayBB47a)

Fernworthy reservoir and intake during a drought in 1949.

(TayP492c)

Sydney Taylor's interest in the ongoing work at Burrator gives an indication of the impact of the engineering project on the public mind, and its effect on Dartmoor. Many photographs in the collection relate to this area over a number of years.

Clockwise from top left: George Shellabeer, water bailiff at Burrator, 1915. New gunmetal valves being fitted at the dam in 1936, with the old valves (centre) which were fitted in 1894. The Princetown railway overlooking the reservoir, 1935. Burrator House, once the home of Sir James Brooke, Rajah of Sarawak – copied by Sydney Taylor from an earlier photograph. The temporary suspension bridge at Burrator, built in 1925 during work to raise the height of the dam.

Bibliography
and further reading

Atkinson et al. *Dartmoor Mines of the Granite Mass,* Exeter 1978

Baldwin et al. *The Book of Manaton,* Halsgrove 1999

Bellamy, Reg. *The Book of Postbridge,* Devon Books 1998

Brears, Peter. *The Old Devon Farmhouse,* Devon Books 1998

Brewer, D. *Field Guide to Boundary Markers on Dartmoor,* Devon Books 1986

Brewer K. *The Railways, Quarries and Cottages of Foggintor,* Orchard, nd

Britton and Brayley. *Devonshire Illustrated,* London 1832

Burnard, Robert. *Dartmoor Pictorial Records,* Devon Books 1986

Butler, Jeremy. *Dartmoor Atlas of Antiquities* Vols 1–5, Devon Books 1991-97

Butler, Jeremy. *Travels in Victorian Devon,* Devon Books 1999

Butler, Simon. *A Gentleman's Walking Tor of Dartmoor,* Devon Books 1986

Butler, Simon. *Dartmoor Century,* Devon Books 1999

Carpenter, Austin C. *Cannon,* Halsgrove 1993

Carter, B. & Skilton B. *Dartmoor: Threatened Wilderness,* Channel 4 1987

Chapman, Chris. *Wild Goose & Riddon,* Halsgrove 2000

Cherry, B. and Pevsner N. *The Buildings of England: Devon,* Penguin 1989

Chugg, Brian. *Victorian and Edwardian Devon,* Batsford 1979

Crossing, William. *Ancient Stone Crosses of Dartmoor,* Devon Books 1987

Crossing, William. *Dartmoor Worker,* Peninsula Press 1992

Crossing, William. *Gems in a Granite Setting,* Devon Books 1987

Crossing, William. *Guide to Dartmoor,* Peninsula Press 1990

Crossing, William. *One Hundred Years on Dartmoor,* Devon Books 1987

Dartmoor National Park Authority. *Guide to Archaeology,* Devon Books 1996

Dartmoor Preservation Association. *A Dartmoor Century,* DPA 1983

Day, Kenneth F. *The Dartmoor Scene,* Frederick Muller 1946

Day, Kenneth F. *Days on Dartmoor,* Devon Books 1987

Fenner, Robin A. *Devon and Cornwall Illustrated,* Stannary Press 1986

Frost, Lee & Robinson Ian. *Dartmoor,* Colin Baxter 1999

Gawne, E. & Sanders, J. *Early Dartmoor Farmhouses,* Orchard 1998

Gill, Crispin. *Dartmoor: A New Study,* David & Charles 1983

Gray, T. & Rowe, M. *Travels in Georgian Devon* (4 vols), Devon Books 2000

Greeves, Tom. *Tin Mines and Miners of Dartmoor,* Devon Books 1986

Griffith, Frances. *Devon's Past: An Aerial View,* Devon Books 1988

Hamilton-Leggett, Peter. *The Dartmoor Bibliography,* Devon Books 1992

Harris, Colin. *Stowford Papermill,* Halsgrove 1999

Harris, Helen. *The Industrial Archaeology of Dartmoor,* David & Charles 1986

Harrison, W. *Dartmoor's Ancient Crosses,* Unpubl.mss

Hemery, Eric. *High Dartmoor,* Robert Hale 1983

Hemery, Eric. *Walking the Dartmoor Waterways,* David & Charles 1986

Hemery, Pauline. *The Book of Meavy,* Halsgrove 1999

Hoskins, W.G. *Devon,* Devon Books 1992

Kingdom, Anthony R. *The Plymouth, Tavistock & Launceston Railway,* ARK Publications 1990

Lauder, Rosemary Anne. *Views of Old Devon,* Bossiney Books 1982

Maxted, Ian (Ed.). *In Pursuit of Devon's History,* Devon Books 1997

Mildren, James. *Dartmoor in the Old Days,* Bossiney Books 1984

Needham, David. *Francis Frith's Devon,* Frith Book Co. 1999

Prince, E. & Head J. *Dartmoor Seasons,* Devon Books 1987

Quick, Tom. *Dartmoor Inns,* Devon Books 1992

Randall-Page, P. & Chapman C. *Granite Song,* Devon Books 1999

Richardson, P.H.G. *Mines of Dartmoor and the Tamar Valley,* Devon Books 1995

Rowe, Samuel. *A Perambulation of Dartmoor,* Devon Books 1985

Sayer, Sylvia. *The Outline of Dartmoor's Story,* Devon Books 1988

Smiles, S. & Pidgley, M. *The Perfection of England,* Exeter 1995

Smith, Martin. *The Railways of Devon,* Ian Allan 1993

Stabb, John. *Devon Church Antiquities,* Simpkin & Marshall 1909

Stanbrook, Elisabeth. *Dartmoor Forest Farms,* Devon Books 1994

Stanes, Robin. *The Old Farm,* Devon Books 1990

Starkey, Harry. *Dartmoor Crosses,* Starkey 1989

Thomas, Peter. *Images of Devon,* Halsgrove 1999

Westlake, Roy. *Dartmoor,* David & Charles 1987

Wills, Dick. *The Book of Ilsington,* Halsgrove 2000

Woodcock, G. *Tavistock's Yesterdays* (10 Vols), Tavistock 1985-1994

Woods, Stephen. *Dartmoor Stone,* Devon Books 1999

Woods, Stephen. *Widecombe - A Pictorial History,* Devon Books 1996

Woods, Stephen. *Widecombe - Uncle Tom Cobley and All,* Devon Books 2000

Specialist works on photography
Baldwin, Gordon. *Looking At Photographs,* Getty/British Museum 1991

Clarke, Graham. *The Photograph,* OUP 1997

Jeffrey, Ian. *Photography,* Thames & Hudson 1981

Pultz, John. *Photography and the Body,* Everyman 1995

Scharf, Aaron. *Art and Photography,* Penguin 1986

Sontag, Susan. *On Photography,* New York 1973

Wells, Liz. *Photography: A Critical Introduction,* Routledge 1998

Index of Photographs

REFERRING TO THE DUAL PHOTOGRAPHS IN THE MAIN BODY OF THE BOOK